HOSPITAL
BEAT

HOSPITAL BEAT

A Police Officer's stories from inside a busy British hospital

Jonathan Nicholas

Matador
5 Weir Road
Kibworth Beauchamp
Leicester LE8 0LQ, UK
Tel: (+44) 116 279 2299
Fax: (+44) 116 279 2277
Email: books@troubador.co.uk
Web: www.troubador.co.uk/matador

ISBN 978 1848767 546

British Library Cataloguing in Publication Data.
A catalogue record for this book is available from the British Library.

Typeset in 11pt StempelGaramond Roman by Troubador Publishing Ltd, Leicester, UK

Printed and bound in the UK by TJ International, Padstow, Cornwall

Matador is an imprint of Troubador Publishing Ltd

PREFACE

I often hear comments as I walk around the hospital in full police uniform. Some of these comments are clearly aimed in my direction, others I overhear as I walk by. Both staff and public sometimes feel the need to remark on my presence. The most common statement from the public, particularly from more elderly people, is, 'Oh, look, a policeman. I wonder what he's doing here...' and comments such as, 'He must be visiting someone.' Others such as, 'Are you lost?' to the most common one, 'It was him..!' as they point to the person next to them, laughing. I have a few stock replies ready such as, 'That's what they all say!' and, 'It's always the one who points at the other, who's actually done it!' or, 'I'll be back for you later then!' and so on, as I walk away, leaving them behind, smiling. A reply is very definitely expected, I know that much. They anticipate one. Not only that, this single encounter with me, at that moment, may possibly be the only encounter they have with a police officer that day, or even that month, year, or indeed, ever. If the public have children with them they almost always make some remark, usually addressing their child with, 'There's a policeman, behave yourself, or he'll take you away,' or similar. Not the most ideal first thoughts for a young child to nurture about police officers. Despite being in an environment where professional public servants abound in huge numbers, and their presence *is* therefore expected, a policeman in full uniform is not. I am a curiosity. I appear to them to be a *non sequitur*. I'm not a doctor or a nurse, so why am I there? Sometimes I *do* stop and tell them, in vague terms, why I am plodding down North Corridor, purposefully and dutifully, as I often do. I've no doubt they *hear* what I say about the various cases of thieving and so on, but I'm quite sure they don't actually *listen*. Are they too shocked to really cope with the realities of what I tell them, or do they simply think I'm making it up? The hospital staff seem more ready to believe me, but I'm sure the public are not.

Hospital dramas on the television are filled with dramatic incidents in emergency rooms, with lots of emotive shouting, fighting, and blood on the floor, which understandably makes for very interesting and exciting viewing. A five month enquiry into a doctor who masturbates at his colleagues, or staff who steal from dying patients, may not make for such good peak-time television. The public would be worried though, if they really knew the scruffy person in the next bed to them was indeed a heroin addict, clearly intent on fleecing them of all their valuables. Perhaps they don't want to know. But people *do* seem interested in my activities at the hospital. This is probably because, like me, they assumed there was little or no crime in a hospital. Crime stops at the gates, doesn't it? Criminals have a code of ethics not to venture into hospital grounds, don't they? A hospital is sacrosanct, a place of safety, isn't it? Well, actually, and very sadly, no. Not all the time. Just like anywhere else, a hospital is fair game, unfortunately. Career criminals, opportunist thieves, dishonest visitors, and a tiny number of dishonest staff of all types and from all departments; they are all here, in this hospital. As they will be in any hospital, anywhere in the world. Dishonesty in modern society is ubiquitous, in every walk of life, from cleaners to Members of Parliament. Many years ago I worked with a young police officer who stole money from the public, and colleagues, at every opportunity. He was rightly dismissed and imprisoned. Once he'd been caught, that is! They never willingly surrender themselves and give up their improbity voluntarily! They would carry on forever, *ad infinitum*, if they could. Someone has to catch them first! In this particular hospital, this task is down to me.

So I will tell you of some of the incidents I have dealt with personally, as a hospital police officer. It is certainly a busy place. There are thousands of people working there, and thousands of visitors, daily. I will tell you a story, of sorts, based on a kind of walking tour of the campus in a roughly clockwise direction, punctuated by my many and varied dealings with the people in it. It's not all bad news and negativity. There's some mildly amusing incidents as well as the crime stories. Crime is not everything a police officer deals with, as you will see. There are some very weird tales to tell, some distressing events, and even some ghost stories! I hope you will be able to get a flavour of the work I have undertaken in the hospital, and also understand how much I've enjoyed doing it. I feel very lucky to have been able to experience the incidents I have described, and feel honoured to have been able to serve the Hospital Trust the way I have. By so doing, I'd like to think I've made this particular hospital a tiny bit safer. I've changed most names to protect the innocent, and guilty. One or two of the incidents have been heavily disguised too, to offer some degree of protection, for those who deserve it, and also for some who don't!

I have stated this book is a story. This is precisely what

it is. It is a work of fiction. But information contained in it is taken from my personal recollections, my police pocket note book, prosecution files, anecdotes and interactions with staff, patients, and offenders, over a six year period. I've written it as a work of fiction in order to avoid having to keep it within the rigid interstices of hard chronological facts. This has given me some freedom to use artistic licence in places where I would perhaps otherwise not have been able to. I wanted to avoid the book reading like a dry, didactic reference book, or training manual, and hopefully more like a series of reasonably interesting incidents. These things I have described do happen in our hospitals. I've no doubt they will be happening in your local hospital too!

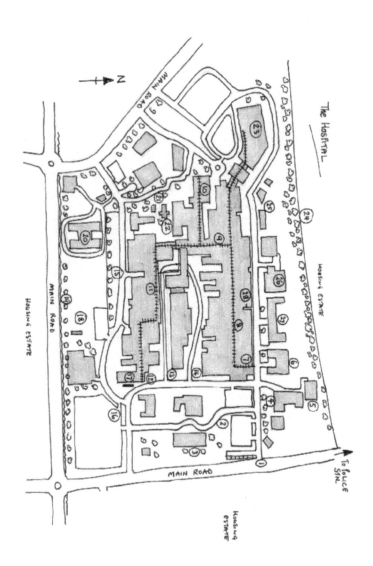

KEY TO MAP:

1. North Road entrance
2. Stabbage Way
3. Laundry
4. Stabbage Lodge
5. Facilities building
6. HQ Building
7. North East Entrance
8. North Corridor
9. X-Ray Corridor
10. Physiotherapy/Outpatients corridor
11. South Corridor
12. East Entrance
13. Service Rd 1
14. Service Rd 2
15. South Road & South car park
16. East Car Park
17. The Dugout
18. Cricket pavilion & cricket pitch
19. The Brook
20. H-Block
21. Chapel Hill
22. The Old Chapel
23. Maternity
24. The North Fence & footpath
25. Doctors' accommodation
26. North Side Restaurant
27. Clinical Sciences
28. The Doctor's Mess

CONTENTS:

NORTH

Walking into the hospital grounds for the first time, in my highly polished, size nine police boots, through the North East Entrance, I was immediately aware North Road was no ordinary street. In my black uniform trousers, bright yellow reflective jacket, and anachronistic pith-helmet style police head gear, I was no ordinary visitor either. I had no idea when I first arrived at this beat area, years ago, such a place as this hospital would cause me to have to deal with quite so many interesting, often alarming, and sometimes shockingly disturbing incidents. In retrospect, I was probably as naïve then, as anyone reading this may be now. I had no idea that in a safe, professional, caring environment such as a hospital, some of the staff would be stealing from colleagues at every opportunity, and even from their unsuspecting, often vulnerable patients. I could never have guessed that some medical professionals enjoyed stealing, and even enjoyed masturbating openly in their coffee breaks, apparently to relieve work-related stress! Local thieves target the hospital because it is never completely locked, and when thieves and drug-addicts become sick, or have babies, they themselves live on the campus temporarily as patients, and steal from others whenever, and wherever they can. But why shouldn't these things happen in a hospital? It is after all, a place where thousands of people attend every day, and so where such a large number of people gather, there will surely be an equally wide gamut of human behaviour. Like

1

anywhere else, there are examples of the very best in human nature, and the very worst. So it is, all of this, that whenever it happens, I have to deal with it. I am the hospital police officer. I am the local sheriff. I'm the Chief Constable of the hospital campus. After so many years, I feel this is now my domain. I am familiar with it, and I know it well. I know some of the people too, and quite a few of the buildings, inside and out. Not all, mind you, but probably a reasonable amount!

So I walk to the hospital almost every day. I almost always choose to use this first entrance as North Road is the nearest to the police station. From beautifully bright, high summer mornings, to the deepest, darkest, and coldest winter days, with all types of weather in between, I've pounded this part of my beat for quite some years.

Looking at its full length, North Road stretches into the near distance, and is physically similar to other roads in the area, of course, if slightly narrower, with the usual street furniture and markings. But it is, however, unlike other, more *ordinary* streets. We are entering a different world, walking into the hospital grounds, specifically, and deliberately separate from the surrounding area. It is a gated, but open community, fenced-off from the outside, but not locked away, with its own unique community identity, and even its own, albeit small, police force of uniformed security staff. The visitor passes the tall, recently re-painted, bright blue, spiked steel fencing at either side of the entrance, where clearly in days past formidable gates once stood. The steel fence of late Victorian construction has been painted and repainted countless times over a century or more; the dried paint runs have runs themselves, and now, without detriment, form part of the texture of the fence. Early past painters of this sturdy old fence must now themselves be long dead memories. The railings are over six feet high and are cold to the touch even on the hottest of days. On the left is a line of a dozen or so newly built town houses set perpendicular to the road; accommodation for hospital staff, located just inside the perimeter fence. Smart, clean, aspirational dwellings filled with equally aspirational medical staff, the majority of whom hail from the Asian sub-continent. Quiet, private and hard working, I have personally encountered very few of these hospital denizens in my numerous visits to the campus. There are no cars on their driveways. Not for them the expensive, shallow status symbols of others. Why should they buy cars, when they live where they work? The rather pretty little tree-lined cul-de-sac is carelessly and wantonly abused by drivers, both public and staff, in order to avoid the car parking levy. They clutter the tiny street with their cars, all day long, and on most days, except at weekends. On the right, and in quite a contrast, a small number of ugly nineteen-seventies town houses sit at a skewed angle to the road across from the new builds. Now only partly occupied, like a forlorn lost ideal, these are rapidly inviting their own demolition. Grass grows madly and energetically in the guttering almost all the way around the roof, clearly neglected for years. Steel poles support flat roofs of car ports, redolent of the time, but no cars shelter there now, just a scattered gang of scruffy, semi-redundant wheelie bins.

'North East' car park on the left. One of the many visitors 'pay and display' car parks. Not cheap. On the right the 'Social Club', behind a short line of perfectly proportioned mature ash trees. Another nineteen-seventies construction no doubt once intended to be a classy establishment, with flat roof, concrete sectional walls, and pebble-dash outer covering. It now more resembles a grimly pretentious northern working men's club, both inside and out. Well, I suppose that is largely what indeed it is. Fit for purpose then. I've not once ventured inside socially, but several times I've visited to take statements from staff and customers. An occasion I remember when a well-known and particularly nasty, brutish local chap and his equally nefarious adult son smashed beer bottles over the head of a male wedding guest, at a reception in the club, then saw fit to use his head briefly, but viciously, as a football. I didn't witness the incident myself, but undertook some of the follow-up enquiries, and sought out the key eye-witness accounts. Both men were eventually given seven years imprisonment for wounding, also known as GBH. Grievous Bodily Harm. It *was* grievous too. The victim almost died. The main protagonist was a typical sort; not particularly large in stature, but having the appearance and attitude which clearly gave an indication of his feckless lifestyle and obnoxious temperament. He was slim, almost wiry, with ubiquitous shaven head, and plentiful scarring on both his face and scalp. Evidence of past disagreements, no doubt. Numerous tattoos, of course, ear-rings, a very fragile ego, and a command of English that would be an insult to many recent Eastern European migrants. Clear evidence of a pitifully poor education, if any at all. He is now deceased, having hanged himself determinedly high up a tree in nearby woods when recently on a single 'day release' from prison, not halfway through the seven year prison term. There's some irony in this. If he'd not been released, as a result of some overly-lenient, no doubt well-intentioned, but hopelessly misguided rehabilitation scheme, he'd still be alive! I'd met him professionally several times before, and once submitted a statement from one of these typically rude and threatening encounters, which I'd written in Hardyesque colloquial language, which went on to be held up as a fine example of the power of the written word. This relatively brief but highly descriptive statement was the sole piece of evidence with which a County Court Judge, no less, granted a two year ASBO on the chap. Power indeed!

The first true hospital building for patients' treatment is on the right adjacent to the Social Club. Stabbage Lodge, a neurological rehabilitation unit, is a single storey building, quite modern, with a very attractive conservatory at the front, facing the road. It is partly obscured by willow screening and trellising, but the wicker furniture, rubber plants, and indoor grasses are still visible inside. Sometimes patients are also seen in their wheelchairs with nursing staff in bright uniforms fussing around them attentively and persistently, like wasps around an apple core on a hot day. I frequently exchange pleasantries with them when on my dutiful wanderings and walkabouts. North Road is then punctuated by a cross-roads, surrendering some linearity as it breaks off right to serve the Facilities building behind Stabbage Lodge, and opposite, left down Stabbage Way. The Facilities building is where I've been a few times to seek the invaluable help of certain genius members of staff who can make the biggest maps you've ever seen. It helps having photocopiers and printers that are so large they must be several yards across, and they make full use of this amazing equipment. I once needed a huge amount of intricate detail on large maps of the campus when I dealt with 'The Flashing Blade' – as I nicknamed him – a doctor who had a rather annoying habit of taking out his erect penis and masturbating at colleagues in his coffee breaks. I *know* everyone has vices, and habits, and even hobbies, but this was way too much! Anyway, I needed detailed plans to plot the routes he took across campus to and from his office, to where he was doing the dirty deed each time. The maps made it all so much easier to follow! More of 'The Flashing Blade' later. The Facilities building is also a single storey with a flat roof. It has some immensely strong convex steel bars over every window, like the ones you see on posh villas around the Mediterranean. No-one can get in either, without buzzing first at the one and only door. Not on a card swipe or digi-lock, you need to be invited in. It has never been burgled.

Stabbage Way leads off to the left and starts to descend, slowly at first, but then with a steep tumble down towards South Road, via a sharp and seemingly rather pointless S-bend. Past the massive factory-sized laundry on the left with the rear of the St Francis wards on the right. I've been to the laundry several times. Loud, steamy and industrious; it smells of a heady mix of sweat, oily old machinery, and cheap, starchy soap powder. Not surprising really, knowing its function! The staff work very hard in almost semi-darkness, with what appears to be some quite antiquated equipment. It's always a warm place where the huge machines clatter and clunk about, pulling at the linen sheets and drawing them through massive rollers like some nightmarish monster dragging its quarry into its mouth with a merciless and ferocious *whoosh!* of heat and steam. One of the very few twenty-four hour buildings on the campus, the staff are a remarkably cheery lot. I was asked to visit as they'd recovered patients' property which had clearly been inadvertently caught up in the bed sheets and pillow cases when sent to the laundry. This had obviously been happening for some time as there was a pile of spectacles quite reminiscent of wartime photos from the Holocaust, only – and respectfully – on a much smaller scale. But almost as sad. The owners may well now be deceased. There were also false teeth, sets and sets of them, old watches the likes of which your grandparents would wear, and some mobile phones. Early mobile phones. The type your children gave to your parents when they had an upgrade. Efforts to find owners must now follow.

THE LADY VANISHES

North east entrance is on the left as we carry on along North Road. Recently moved from the very end of North Corridor, this entrance now has a dog-leg type corridor for an entrance off North Road across a very neat, new car park. This same car park is where an old red brick building once stood, until recently. Such old buildings were common on the hospital campus and have a huge amount of interesting history dating back over a hundred years, some of it quite unpleasant if not a little disturbing; dark paupers cells which looked like medieval dungeons, and dismal Victorian workhouses for the poor. Not to mention the mortuaries and mad houses for the insane. There are some interesting, grainy old black and white photographs of these institutions dotted around the campus, in a celebration of the hospital's recent centenary. The inmates seem to stare out from these photographs, in a parlous state of sadness, and pitiful despondency. These were the places where the deserving, and no doubt some undeserving poor of the time were stored. Rightly or wrongly, they were kept from idleness and forced to earn their keep. They were probably grateful for it too, knowing the alternative at that time. Where the car park is now situated, so once was one of these old historic buildings. And like a lot of these old buildings this one had a history. A rather strange history. It was thought to have been the site of a former mortuary, but one which was attached to a particularly grim 'madhouse'. So many tormented souls would therefore have died in some horrendous circumstances in the old building before more modern and enlightened times. It is known among certain staff that before it was demolished this building was regularly haunted. Probably one or more of these aforementioned lost souls who passed away on the premises. But *haunted*? Yes, I know. I'm with you on this. No one is more sceptical than me when it comes to this subject, but when someone tells you face-to-face they actually witnessed events like this for real, so to speak, and offer themselves up for direct questioning about it – and possible ridicule to boot – then it cannot surely be dismissed out of hand. Can it? So you must decide for yourself if you think what I am about to tell you is the truth. Or not.

The best of these incidents happened when a member of staff – I'll call her Sarah – was coming out of an office on the first floor of the two storey building and was running down the old, but very sturdy staircase. The door at the top was a buzzer-door like the one at the Facilities building, very restricted to certain members of staff only, where one had to be invited in. No-one could get past this door, and it was of a very strong, secure construction. Halfway down the stairs the staircase levelled out briefly onto a landing area, with a bare, concrete floor, before turning back on itself in a hundred and eighty degrees and down towards North Corridor. Sometimes a single chair is placed on such landings in order to assist less able patients to rest on the stairs, but none existed here because, as I said, it was a restricted, 'Staff Only' staircase. On her way down these stairs, in a hurry to collect papers from another office down the corridor, Sarah was surprised to see a very frail- looking elderly lady standing at the small window on the landing, looking out. She had long, straggly, grey hair, a very thin face, and a particularly strange, wistful, and distant look in her eyes, as though deeply troubled, and searching for something far away. She was wearing a shabby, ankle-length night gown the type worn in Victorian times, and nothing at all on her feet. Sarah remembered thinking how cold the floor must have felt to the old lady's feet. She also believes she may have even said 'hello' to her as she rushed past her in haste, without stopping, down the rest of the stairs, and into North Corridor. But then she paused. Still only a few feet, and a few seconds from the bottom of the stairs she stopped, and turned to go back. This lady, she suddenly thought, may be a patient who has lost her way, as often happens, particularly with elderly patients. She must also have remembered her latest 'patient care' staff lectures, and of course her own professionalism, so she ran back up the stairs to speak to her.

She reached the landing area in no time, two steps at a time. She didn't believe what she then saw when she arrived back on the landing. She didn't *want* to believe it. It wasn't possible. The old lady had gone; *completely vanished*. Thinking she must have gone further up the stairs, Sarah looked up to the door at the top, but there was no-one there. The door at the top was clearly locked shut. So was the window, and in any case it was small, locked, and twenty feet up. No-one had come down the stairs after her, either. She had been running anyway, and the old lady couldn't *possibly* have run behind her and gone in that short time. She hadn't seemed capable of *walking*, let alone running. There had to be an explanation. People just do NOT disappear! At the top of the stairs Sarah then asked if anyone had buzzed to go in. No-one had. No-one had gone in that door at all, not for a while, at least. It was then, when she came to an abrupt realization of what she'd just seen, that Sarah states she felt a very, very cold breeze around the stairwell. It was a hot summer's day. How was this possible? When I asked Sarah about this incident, she did not recount the story with any arrogance or animation, but in a rather dispassionate, even prosaic manner. In fact I had to press her to some degree before she would even tell me. She stated she didn't like talking about it. Minutes after it happened, she stated she felt physically sick, and almost went home. She swore on her life it was true. As I said, you will have to judge for yourself, but she has no explanation for this, and if true, neither do I.

On the ground floor of the same building, before it was demolished, security were called out one night. It was a cold winter night, and particularly dark. Two guards were called to someone in the early hours of the morning apparently inside, repeatedly pressing one of the bedside emergency call buttons on the wall. At first they suspected kids had somehow got in, but the ward had been closed, locked, and emptied of beds months before, in preparation for demolition. The two guards arrived at the ward and peered into the blackness through the window in the door. The door was securely locked shut, as were all the other windows. I know these men, and they are not particularly noted for either squeamishness nor inventiveness, but they insist this is exactly what happened: The buzzer inside the ward was being pressed frantically, as if in real desperation, over and over, by someone inside the ward. It seemed very loud, amidst the quiet darkness, and a red light was flashing on the wall, on and off in time to the buzzing sound, towards the back of the ward, to the right. They shone a torch inside and it suddenly, and unexpectedly stopped. There was complete silence. They then remembered, as it was so close to demolition, there was no power of any sort in that part of the building. The buzzer couldn't possibly have worked. They managed to open the door, rather hesitantly, as they later recalled, and walked into the ward. The lights didn't work, as they expected. They walked, close together, in their torchlight, to the area at the back, on the right, where the noise had been coming from. One of them pressed the bedside buzzer on the wall. It didn't make a sound. Sure enough, it wasn't working. Both men later said at that moment they had each wanted to run from that room as fast as they possibly could. Two very well built, very capable security guards! They locked the ward back up and left. This was several years ago. Even now, they won't speak of it, unless asked. Again, no explanation has ever been found.

HQ BUILDING

Across the road from North East entrance is my home-from-home on the campus, a tall old building in a U shape facing the road called Nurses Home Two. It was once nurses accommodation, as the name suggests but, now very tastefully refurbished, it has been converted to rather smart offices. Senior management have moved in, including the Hospital Chief Executive and his staff. The building is now known as the Hospital HQ. The best part of the refurbishment, in my opinion, is the way the old parquet wood floor has been revealed from under decades of dirt and grime, sanded, and restored to full glory, with the beautiful wood grain visible once more. It's a pleasure to walk on! The ground floor is where security have their offices. Along the corridor I have an office too. The new security control room is a place of beguiling complexity and resembles the bridge of a star ship. There are a dozen huge flat screen plasma CCTV monitors all down one wall which can be set to split-screen, multi-screen, roaming, near-shots, distance-shots, and seemingly anything else you could wish for. To the layman, a nightmare, but to the staff operating it, easy. Virtually the whole campus is covered by at least one of the many digital cameras across the site. Some of these cameras sit high on the tops of buildings for all to see, with panoramic views, but some corridor cameras are so tiny they are virtually undetectable, and mostly go completely unseen. The quality of the images from all of these cameras is remarkable, along with the new technology which governs them. The staff in there are pretty good too! I've known most for years, and we have a happy, mutually exploitative working relationship. We exchange information as representatives of 'partner agencies' and work well together. Rarely, if ever, would I visit the campus and not call in, even briefly.

Next to this is the Clinical Sciences building; not been in there very much, I have to say. Quite new, tall and smart looking, with lots of tinted glass and exposed steel, it stands there looking like a more prosperous, arrogant cousin of the surrounding buildings. It has a very swish foyer and reception area resplendent with expensive-looking leather, and highly polished floors, which wouldn't go amiss in any smart London hotel. It's an office block full of people I've never met. I'm not likely to ever meet them either. There's rarely any crime there, and I have no need of their services, whatever they are. Next door is the North Side Restaurant. This is the main restaurant which serves the whole campus and feeds hundreds on a suitably industrial scale. It's really a large canteen – rather than a restaurant – with dozens of tables in a communal, kibbutz-style dining room. Bright, and flooded with light from huge windows on three sides, and skylights lined across the ceiling in a chess-board fashion. The quality of the cooking can be remarkably variable, but is usually good basic culinary fare, and a 'five item' English breakfast of sausage, bacon, tomatoes, mushrooms, and an egg currently sets you back £1.80.

HQ Building

THE MANY DOORS OF DR CHU

Opposite Clinical Sciences is the Main Entrance. There's an ambulance bay adjacent to it, and a large, open doorway area, with long, wide straggly bits of thick, clear plastic hanging down over it, like heavy Dorset kelp. A short walk into the Main Entrance takes you into North Corridor. On the right as you walk into this entrance there are three doors at the end of another, much shorter corridor, one of which leads up stairs to the Doctor's Mess. At the top of the stairs there's yet another door onto a landing area. Finally there's a door leading directly into the doctor's mess room. The doors at the foot of the stairs are of good quality and governed by ID card swipe locks. So are the ones at the top. Only staff could therefore gain access. But this would also include cleaners, known on campus as 'domestics.' So far the one and only time I've ever been summoned to this department was when the department manager reported a large expensive item 'missing' from the mess. The missing item was a new forty inch plasma television, complete with cabinet stand and smoked glass doors. Nothing had apparently been disturbed, no doors or windows had been damaged, and there were no signs of any forced entry at all. Very mysterious indeed. The missing items were so new in fact, that the cardboard boxes they'd arrived in were still in the room! Rather optimistically at that stage, when I first arrived at the scene, I ripped part of the box away on which the serial number was written, in case I found the tv on my travels. I slotted this piece of cardboard in the folds of my pocket book. There were two young male doctors seated on a sofa, occasionally glancing in my direction, tapping away on their lap-top computers. Both looked as if they were barely clear of their teens. I introduced myself to the caller, the department manager, Dr Sally Roberts, now standing before me, and began to take details.

Sally was in her late twenties, very tall and slim, and was unusually – I thought – wearing a lot of very, very bright red glossy lipstick. Too much, really. Any more and she'd start to look a bit like a clown. She had straight black shiny hair in a bob which hugged her fine, slender neck, and a thin, rather harsh-looking face, which was utterly transformed and lit up when she smiled. Hence the lipstick, I suppose. Or because of it! She was wearing a perfectly tight, knee-length pencil-skirt which showed her curves beautifully. She had a stethoscope around her neck. A lot of the doctors do. Most probably a status symbol. Like a large bunch of keys to some people, or a mobile phone in the days when they were new, and they were carried overtly, on the belt, in a leather pouch. It was then I began to work out how someone could possibly take such a massive tv complete with stand, undetected. I know it's wrong to blame cleaners every time something goes missing, and I don't *every* time, but they *are* sometimes my first thought. They can access everywhere, are not well paid, and they can often be temporary agency staff, with no loyalty to the department, or even the hospital. They frequently clean when everyone else has gone home, too, so temptation may exist over and above normal circumstances. But the doctors' mess is open twenty-four hours so a doctor could potentially walk in at any moment. Another possibility was that staff from another ward or department had seen the new delivery, and took it upon themselves to 'borrow' the items, without informing the manager. This has been known to happen before in other departments. I asked Sally to make enquiries with other senior colleagues, and also asked her to announce an amnesty, should someone want to bring the items back. It had quite obviously been taken by someone with lawful access to the room, judging by the number of secure doors which needed to be passed, none of which were damaged. A member of staff then. If it was committed to paper, and an arrest followed, I knew the hospital Trust may push for dismissal. It would mean the probable end of someone's medical career. So I left the matter for around forty-eight hours, and returned to the scene.

On my return, Sally stated she'd heard nothing, and she was now getting concerned, as I was. I allocated a crime number and began enquiries. No turning back now. I stomped thoughtfully across North Road and into the security office. The card swipe system is recorded on a database. Thousands of transactions every day. I sat down with one of the staff and we started scanning the system. There were a huge number of swipe transactions and doors to isolate and check. But specifically the area around the doctors' mess, and all its associated doors that previous weekend. After almost two hours we found it. Three doors had been propped open for ten minutes at around 1 a.m. the previous Saturday night. Then again about twenty minutes later. And opened again, but briefly that time. Someone had been very busy with the doors at the top and bottom of the stairs to the doctors' mess. The main entrance doors had also been propped open for a while too. The swipe was identified, and the current holder was a member of staff: Dr Yuan Chu.

I confirmed there had not been any reports of that particular ID card being lost or stolen, then I grabbed a colleague and went to make a home visit to the doctor. We had a twenty-five minute drive out of the city, north, to a small town known to my colleague, Gary, as it was his home town. As a result, we found the doctor's address relatively easily and parked the van outside. We'd brought the small Ford Connect van. Handy, with a small cage in the back in which to place our captives. There was a tall set of spike-topped steel gates at the end of the driveway. They were locked. We climbed over the six foot wall at the side of the gates, and landed heavily in the garden, like a pair of very unfit paratroopers. We walked up the driveway and approached his front door. I knocked loudly, and also pressed the doorbell. The doctor approached and saw us through the frosted glass in the door. I could see him hesitating. He opened the door, in obvious reluctance, and we stepped inside. After formal introductions I walked into his living room. There it was, all plugged in, set on the cabinet with the smoked glass doors. I walked over and took out my little bit of cardboard. Not that I needed it, but the serial numbers were an exact match.

Dr Chu was a slight fellow, not very tall, slim, in his early thirties, and wearing black, square-rimmed spectacles, a bit like those trademark glasses worn by Sir Michael Caine. They looked way too big for him, to be honest, and he appeared a little comical as a result. But under these circumstances, the dichotomy was that he also looked sad and pathetic. I asked him where the television came from. He didn't answer, but turned his head down towards the floor. He held his hands together in front of him. I could see the upright stature of his frame slowly but perceptibly shrinking away like ice-cream in summer sun, as I asked him again. Then the most extraordinary thing happened. He collapsed to his knees in front of me, onto his thick, white shag-pile rug, right in front of the stolen television, and started moaning and groaning, over and over:

"Please... please... *please*...I'm sorry... I'm sorry... please... *pleeeeaaase!!*"

He started crawling towards me on all fours, in a cloyingly subservient grovel, his face an inch from the floor, not looking up at all. I considered moving back, but there was nowhere for me to retreat to. What if he lunged at me and attacked me? When he finally reached my feet he started caressing and fondling my size nine police boots with his bony, thieving little hands, putting greasy finger marks all over my lovely polished toe-caps. My colleague and I looked at each other in utter bewilderment and consternation. I didn't know what to say, but of the two of us, Gary spoke first:

"Perhaps he just wants us to give him a damned good shoeing, take the telly, and leave it at that?"

Perhaps he did, I don't know. I ended up taking hold of him and pulling him up to his feet, only for him to drop back to the floor, limp, like a corpse. I heard myself sounding like a concerned parent when a child falls over:

"Get up, get up, we're not going to hurt you, you know," and almost felt like saying, 'There, there, it'll be alright...'

We spent the next half-hour searching his ground floor flat while he was crouched double on his knees the whole time on the floor, as though about to throw himself into a forward roll. The moaning had faded to a dull murmuring by now but still continued, over and over:

"Please... please... pleeeeease!"

We searched his bedroom and when we came back out I nearly fell over him, as he was now huddled over, moaning, in the hallway, having moved from the lounge . I wondered if he'd crawled, or got up and walked. In all my service to date no-one has ever offered me a bribe. It occurred to me then, though, that he may have considered such a thing as a favourable outcome to his predicament. But he didn't, thankfully. (Besides, at what price would I set myself? I'd never really given it any serious thought!) We bundled him into the cage in the back of the van, put the television and stand on the back seat, and drove back to base. You know those occasions from childhood, usually in school, when you are forbidden to laugh, and so it becomes even funnier? The drive back to the nick that day for Gary and I was truly one of those occasions.

Dr Chu maintained his obsequious demeanour the whole time he was in custody. I couldn't work out whether it was all an act, or maybe something deeper, or even cultural. He rarely made eye-contact with anyone, and was so softly spoken most of the time no-one could hear a word he said. He repeated his chanting over and over again, this time to the custody sergeant, who actually had to tell him, as politely as he possibly could, to stop apologising. 'I'm sorry, but could you stop apologising please?' He was the polar opposite of many drunken, abusive, loud and aggressive persons more commonly brought before him. While he was being booked into custody I drove down to the hospital with Gary and returned the television and stand. Dr Roberts was delighted, of course. She was understandably shocked when I told her who had taken it. She knew the chap, though not very well. She said he'd always seemed a bit moody, and quiet, not mixing a great deal with other staff.

I was very happy to be able to return the property, as I always am in these circumstances. It's a very satisfying experience after so many other occasions when the property seems to vanish, never to be seen again. I know this may sound a bit cheesy, but it makes *us* look good too, the *police service* as a whole, when we have a relatively quick success like this. We so often get a bad press, it's genuinely nice to be able to help in this way , to arrive at such a successful conclusion.

When we returned to the station we took Dr Chu from his cell. He was an ideal interviewee. He happily and frankly admitted stealing the television (what choice did he have?!) despite earning five thousand pounds a month, and therefore having plenty of money to buy the equivalent from the shops any time he wanted. I think most of the twenty minute interview tape consisted of both him apologising constantly, and me telling him to stop apologising. God only knows what it must have sounded like, played back. He had no real substantive explanation or excuse for doing what he did other than he just wanted it. He described in detail how he'd propped all the doors open with chairs, and carried the television to his car. He had to partly dismantle the stand to get it down the stairs, it was so cumbersome and awkward. He took a great risk doing this that night. Maybe this was part of the reason he took it. The fact the property was recovered, intact, and undamaged, of course went in his favour. Even though it was I who'd recovered it. After adding to this his 'previous good character', it was decided he should be given an 'Adult Caution', and avoid court. This sounds lenient, I know. But he's had his fingerprints, DNA, and photograph taken, and he now has a PNCID (Police National Computer Identity Number, issued to everyone arrested). A police record. Theft from employer. I sent along copies of my evidence to the hospital, under the umbrella of our 'information sharing protocol', for their internal discipline hearing. As far as I know, I believe he kept his job, just. But he was moved. Anyway, the next day Gary and I, and all the uniform officers in the station, tucked into a large tin of 'Quality Street' chocolates left for us at the enquiry counter with a note. It was from Dr Chu. It just said: "I'm sorry, I'm sorry. Thank you, I'm sorry."

E.A.U

North Corridor runs from the north east entrance at one end, right through to maternity at the other, probably several hundred yards long. From my perspective, in summer it's hot and stifling, and in winter, warm and dry. There are many wards and departments either side of most of this corridor. I would guess I've visited every one of them, at some time or another. Not always for crime-related issues, but for any number of things. I will recount a particular incident though, which was very much crime-related. It took me a fair amount of my time and numerous visits to the department in order to resolve the problem. E.A.U. stands for Emergency Admissions Unit. It is now based on South Corridor but for this occasion it was still on North. It was near the main entrance and the ambulance bay. I was called to the unit by the ward manager, who I shall call Karen. By the way, 'ward manager' is now the modern euphemism for 'matron'; the type played so well by Hattie Jacques in the old 'Carry On' films. For some of them quite an accurate stereotype, but not, I have to say, in this instance. I accompanied Karen to her office and she shut the door behind us. Karen was a good-looking woman not in the least bit austere, or fat, but discreetly and sweetly attractive, even sexy. In her thirties, she had thick shoulder-length blonde hair, tied back, and quite amazing sea-green eyes. She told me of quite a large number of minor thefts which had been happening in the ward for several months, and probably throughout the whole year. Cash, mainly, but lately and more worryingly, wallets and purses, from both staff and patients. A veritable multiplicity of petty thieving. A bit of minor theft between staff is one thing, but when it gravitates to the patients, then somehow the offender has truly crossed the Rubicon. Whoever it was, was now well and truly taking the pee.

At first Karen was quite equivocal in her account and I could sense a degree of understandable reticence on her part to reveal her true suspicions. But I could also sense there was some desperation in her voice which must have, after all, been the prompt for her to ring me in the first place. Karen had thankfully recorded the times and dates of all the thefts quite meticulously, and completed the necessary incident forms very thoroughly. I started scanning these and occasionally as I did so, another member of staff would open the door suddenly, only to see us both deep in thought, poring over the reports, before apologising and leaving. I asked to see the staff duty rotas and Karen stood up to reach a shelf above her desk. She was probably almost six feet tall in her flat shoes, and her typical blue and white nurses uniform fitted where it touched her slim figure. As she reached for the lever-arch file, her uniform rose up a few more inches, revealing a pretty decent pair of legs. She was only a foot or so from my face as I sat at a right angle to her on a moulded plastic chair next to her desk. I could smell her cleanliness. I could see close up the crispness of the creases in her skirt, the hem of which was just touching the skin on her left thigh. She dropped the heavy folder onto the desk, completely shattering my shamefully lecherous Reggie Perrin moment.

I was shocked by the scale of the thieving, as so much had gone completely unreported, to the police at any rate.

Going back around twelve months, patients had initially reported small sums such as five pounds and ten pounds missing. But now fifty and a hundred pound sums were being stolen. The latest crime, only that week, was much worse; an old chap called Harry Robertson, had his debit card with his PIN number, stolen from his wallet by his bed. A thousand pounds had been taken from his account in four separate withdrawals of two hundred and fifty pounds. It was getting serious and the thief was getting greedy. Opening the heavy file of duty rotas, each week was on a page neatly covered in a plastic sleeve. I waded through them. As I did so I was offered a cup of coffee and Karen briefly disappeared. On her return a few minutes later with the coffee, I remarked out loud what I had really been thinking privately. We needed to catch this person urgently. After a while I'd managed to compile a short list of four names, common to a lot of the crimes. Then three. Then two. Then only one name was common to every single theft. This person didn't work Christmas, the summer, or any other school holidays, or even weekends. There were no thefts at these times either. Not a single one. Even when this person had random days off there were no thefts. But on her return to work, on each occasion, the thefts started again. There was only one person. An auxiliary nurse by the name of Cheryl Bawtry.

I suggested this name to Karen. She immediately said:

"Yes. That's who I think it is too."

She'd obviously been waiting for me to come to the same conclusion as she had.

"How long have you suspected her?" I asked, still holding my list of names.

"Quite some time now. At least the last few weeks," she said, now in a more reassuringly positive tone.

The circumstantial evidence was compelling. I gathered the necessary documents and returned to base. I then drove down to the magistrates court and obtained a search warrant for Bawtry's home address. When arresting a suspect for acquisitive crime such as this, the law allows police to search the suspect's home on arrest, provided entry has been gained, usually by consent. On occasions, and for certain searches, waiting for the door to be opened can cause precious moments to pass, moments when evidence could be disposed of. A warrant entitles the police to smash the door in – if necessary – quickly and instantaneously, thereby ensuring the best possible chance to recover evidence. I didn't know what to expect at Bawtry's house. I couldn't risk being told to "Fuck off!" through the letter box, as happened on other, similar occasions, and end up with egg on my face and no evidence. Finding stolen property in a persons' address is the very best evidence.

Myself and half a dozen colleagues drove over to Bawtry's house at six a.m. I was shocked to find it was a smart, middle-class detached house, in a respectable area of the city. She was clearly not suffering an impecunious existence of any kind. I knocked on the door. Gary was poised with the 'enforcer' – a very heavy lump of steel with handles and painted bright red – ready to attack the UPVC door. It was opened quickly however, by a well dressed , and well-spoken chap who I assumed, correctly, was the husband. He was understandably very shocked to see so many uniformed police officers on his doorstep! I handed him a copy of the warrant and made the necessary introductions. Cheryl was sitting at a round, varnished pine table in the kitchen, cup of tea in hand. On seeing me, she immediately started shaking, as if suddenly thrust into an icy breeze on a winter's day. I remember at that point I bent over and whispered something in her ear that only she could hear. It was very unprofessional of me, but I said to her:

"How long did you think it would take before we caught up with you?"

She said nothing, and continued shaking, but now even more so. She didn't look at me. Or anyone else.

After forty-five minutes I was very worried as we hadn't found anything incriminating. We searched all the rooms in the house, the shed, the car, the garage, and even the loft. Nothing. I was beginning to think we may have the wrong person. How could I even think that? Would I now come to regret what I'd rather stupidly, and arrogantly, said to Bawtry when we went into the house, or *even* have to *apologise* to her? I was about to call everyone together in order to make preparations to leave, when a female PCSO colleague, Kelly, noticed Bawtry had a hand bag on the floor between her feet, under the table. She was clearly making efforts for us to avoid seeing it. Kelly asked her to lift it up onto the table. Kelly then took hold of it and passed it to me. I opened it. Inside was Mr Robertson's *NatWest* debit card. Bawtry's head bowed. She stared at the floor in genuflection, a sullen, elegiac expression on her face.

She didn't say a great deal in subsequent interviews. In fact she was very far from loquacious the whole time she was in custody. She was quiet and subdued, reluctantly subsumed to the sudden change I'd brought about her life. The look of vilification in her eyes on the rare occasions she looked my way spoke volumes.

It turned out her particular *modus operandi*, or 'MO' as we call it, was to specifically target elderly patients. She would then find a pretext to search their bags or wallets, as she guessed older people would probably have their PIN numbers written on a scrap of paper with their debit cards. Quite often she was right, as in the case of dear old Harry Robertson. Mr Robertson died before I could bring him the good news. Sadly, police are not allowed to make reference to it at court as it is deemed to be inadmissible under rules of evidence, but once Bawtry had been taken out the equation, the thieving in that part of the hospital completely stopped. Having been immediately suspended from duty, then dismissed, eventually, at Crown Court, she was given a twelve month suspended prison sentence. Oh, and front page news in the local newspaper!

BOBBY

Halfway along North Corridor on the left is West Corridor, better known colloquially as X-Ray Corridor. Down here on the right is Physiotherapy corridor which runs to the entrance of the same name. This area of the hospital accommodates a lot of the administration offices for the nearby departments. Usually quite small but numerous, with only three or four staff in each. These staff had a habit of propping their doors open and abandoning their offices for smoke breaks, coffee breaks, and even hour-long lunch breaks. Easy pickings therefore for an opportunist thief.

In common with a lot of thieves, and probably because his local hospital was a public place, always open and available, to Bobby Todd, everything in it that wasn't permanently nailed to the floor was considered *res nullius*, and free for the taking. It was generally known that things would 'disappear' if Bobby had been seen around, and staff seemed to have resigned themselves to the two things happening together, in parallel, but never quite making the obvious connection between them. In fact the hospital had been preyed upon by him for years. Probably as long as he'd been addicted to heroin. He had just about become part of hospital folklore he'd been seen on the campus so often. He seemed to see himself as some sort of 'cheeky chappy' character, and was well known to numerous members of staff in as many departments. Typically thin, almost emaciated, no doubt the result of his long-term habit, in his mid-thirties, he was always unshaven and filthy, apart from the regular occasions he was up before the beak on one of his many sob-story outings to court. To me, he did not possess a single redeeming feature. He was simply a scruffy, thieving, pernicious little bastard. A career criminal in the truest sense. A pioneer and standard bearer of the Great British Underclass, so aptly described by the likes of the equally great Charles Murray and Theodore Dalrymple .

Bobby would normally content himself with stealing small, easily portable objects, such as hand- bags, wallets, and mobile phones from offices and desks, and perhaps the odd charity collection tin. He would spend several hours a day wandering around the campus searching out his opportunities. I really believe it was almost a job to him. Utterly empirical, therefore, in his approach to crime, he developed a thoroughly enviable and intricate working knowledge of the whole campus. When the hospital re-building programme commenced a few years ago, in the boom years for the NHS, there opened up huge opportunities for thieves, and so quickly became an absolute boon to Bobby's nefarious criminal activities. There were dozens of builders and tradesmen on the campus wandering about all over the place. They didn't need to wear ID and no-one would challenge them. Bobby therefore acquired for himself – most probably by theft from these very people – a hard hat, a pair of work boots, and a reflective yellow jacket. He could now slither around the whole site with total impunity. He changed his tactics as a result, and became more ambitious. But by so doing, he made himself an easier target in the process. We started receiving complaints of computers being stolen. Whole systems, including the hard drive, flat screen monitors, and keyboards, were being stolen from offices in the daytime. Someone had been walking in and just unplugging them, and walking straight out again. A written weekly tally of computer thefts suddenly became *de rigueur*, and the incidents were alarmingly ubiquitous across the whole campus. And the situation was rapidly worsening.

It didn't take long before we had some CCTV footage of Bobby captured in a suspicious incident. He had been recorded walking down X-Ray corridor one lunch time with what appeared to be an empty carrier bag in one hand. A few minutes later he was seen walking back up the same corridor with something square, bulky and heavy in the same bag. We could see he was entering and leaving the campus via a hole in the fence at the rear of North Side Restaurant. Like a verminous rat squeezing in and out of a garden shed. It couldn't have been easier for him: he lived in the council flats just the other side of the fence, up a bit of steep, muddy bank. In fact his first floor flat was the very *closest* to the hole in the fence. Search warrant in hand, we paid him a visit at six a.m. one late autumn morning. It's always this early. It's a police tradition!

I don't think I'd be entirely disingenuous in comparing people such as Bobby to insects like cockroaches. They feed off others in a typically parasitic and carelessly ebullient manner, consider nothing sacrosanct, and their only interest in their miserably tedious and feckless existence is the pursuit of their own hedonistic ends, at whatever cost, regardless of such encumbrances which hinder the rest of us, such as moral scruples. I can't begin to imagine the level of free thought which goes on in the head of such a rapacious person, so apparently at liberty to do whatever they wish, whenever they wish, all at the expense of their fellow law-abiding citizens. Like Premiership footballers.

We boshed Bobby's door in, in an instant, with our big red key, the 'enforcer' (we nick-named it our 'bosher', hence the term!). We didn't bother to knock. We rarely do when we have our big red key.

The smell is the first thing that hits you in a flat occupied for years by the likes of him. It wafts over you like an invisible fetid wave, and the heat – it's always stiflingly hot – as when the aircraft door is opened after landing in the tropics. Months or even years of undisturbed body odour, unwashed clothes, scruffy human beings, stale tobacco smoke, old food waste, dirt, and faeces. Layers of dust and grime burns away on the gas fire, usually set to full on. They always have a menagerie of pets they simply can't cope with too, their foul excrement over time pressed solidly and irretrievably into the threadbare carpets and cheap, badly fitted linoleum. And very little light; they like the curtains permanently drawn to create the dark, dismal, cave-like atmosphere they seem to cherish. There was a lot of shouting, screaming even, and a lot of running about. I stepped over piles and piles of dirty clothes that were everywhere on the floor. Suddenly in one of the gloomy bedrooms, I saw a thin, pasty white figure of a male, dressed only in a pair of off-white, and very baggy Y-fronts, in silhouette, climbing out of a window. It was Bobby. We were at least fifteen feet above ground in his flat. It didn't deter him. I ran down the urine-soaked concrete stairwell, three steps at a time, and out of the door. He'd gone. *Mea culpa* . We – or rather I – should have been more prepared. It was *my* search warrant and therefore *my* mistake.

On searching the flat we found a hospital computer under one of the piles of dirty clothes. I also found a hospital laminator and a telephone, complete with answer-machine. We caught Bobby a day later, and he was interviewed – denying everything of course – and bailed. Reports of him on the hospital campus continued, however, despite bail conditions to keep away. How dare he breach those bail conditions! His arrogance in ignoring the conditions imposed on him was a true reflection of his irredeemable fecklessness and the depths of his solipsism. So we paid Bobby another visit. On this occasion when he jumped out of a window, the bathroom window this time, we were ready. He jumped into the arms – and handcuffs – of a colleague. Dressed in only the same scruffy and disgusting underpants, we put him in the cage in the back of the van. I seem to remember it was dark and particularly cold that morning, around minus four degrees, and sadly there was no heating in the back of the van. Unfortunately therefore, Bobby had to sit for over an hour in that awfully cold cage while we searched his flat again. 'Oh dear, how sad, never mind', as Windsor Davies used to say.

That particular winter we visited Bobby's flat four times in all. On each occasion we found hospital property, mainly IT equipment and electrical items. On the last of the four visits, instead of trying to escape himself, we caught him standing on his filthy mattress, hurriedly shoving hospital property out of his bedroom window, in an utterly futile attempt at self-preservation, to fall down below onto the grass outside. A computer base unit and a fax machine were launched out of the window by his pale, asthenic, pipe-cleaner arms, smashing to pieces as they dented the turf, narrowly missing colleagues prepared for more human, Y-fronted contraband. His girlfriend and step-son were present on each of our visits. Selena would probably look quite reasonable if she ever had a wash of any sort, but the filthiness of her teeth were only matched by the filthy and disgusting language which came out of her mouth on each occasion. She was slim and had shoulder-length, blonde hair. Probably. It was knotted, greasy, and unkempt, as though once knitted eons ago in a dark room by a blind orang-utan. It was in these surroundings and by these parents, that her eleven year old son Leon was growing up. On every visit he was happy to offer us a litany of insults in an obvious, apparently genuine, and intensely execrable hatred of police officers. I know no-one loves coppers, I realise this, but really, he was way over the top! Even at that time, and at that age, he was on bail for house burglary. Nature or nurture? It will only be a few short years hence until he's having offspring of his own. If he hasn't already produced some.

I've often found that thieves pitch their crimes at a certain level at which they can accept their activities according to their own conscience. Most people would accept a free ride on a bus or a tram, if the conductor genuinely couldn't get to them in time to make payment. And it would be far too awkward and rude to push your way through the crush to get to him. You know it's wrong, but everyone does it, don't they? So it's alright, isn't it? You know you would pay, if asked. But to actually *steal* something? Even faced with convincing hospital CCTV evidence Bobby would never admit stealing anything from the hospital campus. At first he even tried claiming all the hospital property found in his flat were items he'd found *outside* his flat on the grass! Including the ones he'd launched so ridiculously out of the window as we watched. He even stated he was 'just about to hand it in to the police station...' but that we'd beaten him to it, so we saved him the job. So it was that he finally admitted some offences. He admitted Handling Stolen Goods, on all the four occasions. He just couldn't admit stealing from the hospital. Even though the 'handling' offences carry greater penalties. He went to Crown Court, but he was only given a suspended sentence. This was a huge disappointment, as it meant he was still on the scene. Eventually though, we did get rid of him, so to speak. He was later discovered – amazingly enough – illegally sub-letting his grotty council flat, and was evicted by the housing authority. They really do not like their tenants sub-letting! A colleague and I watched him as he and Selena and Leon trudged despondently off our area together, one morning in pouring rain. They carried what they could of their dirty clothes and possessions, in black plastic bin bags, looking for all the world like a luckless family of disparate refugees. *Stercus accidit*, Bobby, old chap.

COFFEE

X –Ray corridor has one of the four, and in my humble opinion, the best, of the coffee shops on the campus. Though identical, and selling an identical selection of food and drink, this is my favourite. The biggest reason must be its location. It is situated geographically in the centre of the campus. From there, nowhere is too far away. I quite often sit on one of the bar stools sipping my latte, while scribbling in my pocket book, or fiddling with my police Blackberry. I sometimes imagine I'm not there at all, but in a pavement cafe somewhere in Provence, as I was, briefly, the previous summer. Not easy though, when every now and then someone would see me, and quite suddenly say:

"Oh, 'ello duck. Nice to see a policeman 'ere!", and so on.

I was once called to this coffee shop when security had found a 'suspicious bag' on the floor, leant up against a bin. It was right in the middle of the busiest and usually most congested part of the coffee shop. It was therefore ideally placed. The immediate area had been evacuated and the coffee shop closed. I'd walked into the security office, quite by chance, when the next precautionary stage was about to be implemented. The bomb squad were to be called in. I knew something of what that would entail. A full evacuation of that side of the hospital. A huge, very time-consuming and expensive exercise. So I strode purposefully down x-ray corridor to meet the challenge. On arrival I found the area already deserted. It would normally have been extremely busy. Then I saw the bag. A small black back-pack. I turned my radio off. Apparently the radio waves can trigger some devices. I took off my helmet and laid it down next to the bag. I took out my spectacles and carefully put them on. I knew the chances of it being a real device were slim. Who on earth would want to blow up this hospital? But there *was* a possibility it was genuine. It *did* cross my mind that if it was real, and it exploded, would I actually know anything about it? Probably not. All I did know was that no-one else was willing to go near it, let alone investigate it. So it was down to me. Or I could have left it for the 'bomb squad'. Should I? Perhaps I ought to, just to be on the safe side? Sod that, I thought. So I crouched down on the cold floor, and started to unzip the main compartment of the bag. I pulled slowly at the main zip and it moved effortlessly and smoothly until the bag was wide open, like a gaping, toothless mouth. So far so good. I leaned across it, and peered inside. I saw a towel, white and blue, folded over, on the top. I reached in and pulled it out, slowly. Then a pair of clean underpants. Mens. Then a torch. A can of deodorant. And a shirt. That was it. No ticking parcel or sticks of dynamite with wires attached. Nothing that would have exploded. Not this time. Back to my latte, and my Blackberry.

My Blackberry has been provided for me, free, by my employers, and is part of the police drive for 'mobile technology', as it is called. I would have thought anything with a battery in it, that you could feasibly carry with relative ease, could be called 'mobile technology'. Never mind. It's the thought that counts, as they say! I am of course very grateful for anything provided for me for nothing. It's intended to replace the hand-written pocket note book. The only snag with this idea though, is, for the time being, I have to keep both, in parallel, because I prefer my tried and tested pocket book. It doesn't need a battery. But then I'm old. I've yet to experience standing there in the witness box, in court, for all the world utterly alone, while trying vainly to maintain an appreciable air of professional aplomb, and begging the court 'May I please refer to my Blackberry?' Technology is here to stay though, so it's pointless trying to fight it. I've had it over a year now. I'm getting used to it. I can access all the necessary police computer systems through it. Intelligence systems, crime recording systems, and the first, and best system we have, in my opinion, the PNC. The Police National Computer. Millions of names, and millions of vehicle details, all at my fingertips. Also, I can access my emails. So it *can* be useful! Oh, and it's a phone too. And a camera! Though not a very good one (only 3.2 megapixel). I admit I find it beguiling and frustrating in equal measure. I tolerate it and feel the need to subdue it, probably because of my age, like a bad habit that lingers, despite my churlish efforts to be rid of it. As a habit, I'd rather not have it. Like smoking or picking my nose. I have in the past launched into a rather childish and bitter condemnation of what I saw as a profligate waste of cash, these things ever being issued to us in the first place. But now, rather grudgingly, such polemical rhetoric, from me at least, is confined to the times when the battery goes flat, seemingly with little warning. When this happens, I cradle my little Blackberry in my hand, while it seems to gaze incredulously back up at me, like a once loved, but thoroughly mistrusted family pet, now finally dying in my arms. As it fades away on its last breath, it gathers together a final spark of life to tell me, rather belligerently

I feel, in some weedy, thin red script '*You have insufficient battery life*'. *I* have insufficient battery life? Shouldn't it surely say: 'I'm very sorry, mate, but I'm knackered, so I'm going to sleep. This is because YOU haven't charged me for days, you daft old plonker!' It seems to tolerate masses of abuse from me, poor thing, and carelessness (I've dropped it a few times), but it continues to serve. I'll never be rid of it.

As I sit on my bar stool I sometimes make assessments of the various crimes and incidents visited that day. With occasional interaction with Joe Public, I probably appear wildly out of place in my all-black uniform and bullet-proof vest. Charged up with caffeine, and pocket book up to date, I would then move on to the next challenge.

X-RAY

A little further down X-Ray corridor, not far from the coffee shop, and on the same side of the corridor, there is a very discreet, window-less door marked 'Chapel of Rest'. There's a buzzer to press, which looks like someone's home doorbell, but with 'Press for Attention' written above it, on a small plastic sign screwed to the door. It is not just a chapel of rest though. This is also the hospital mortuary. There are a total of seventy-two large, open-sided, sliding drawers, constantly chilled, and usually between a third, and half of them, are occupied most of the time. There are seasonal changes to the occupancy rates, similar to a seaside boarding house; in summer customer numbers increase sharply, as the sick and elderly suffer more chronic breathing problems in hot weather. Then of course there are the problems associated with winter, and other health issues related to it, and elderly people dying of the cold. We are one of the richest countries in the world and yet many of our fellow citizens often die from lack of basic heating in their homes. There's no great mystery around dead people. Just sadness and a reminder of our own mortality. They just lie there, cold, clammy and quiet, minding their own business.

Not everyone admitted to the hospital passes away there, of course. Terminally ill patients are allowed home wherever possible, to end their days in their familiar home surroundings. The deceased are checked for valuables, and any which remain with them are gathered together, bagged and tagged, in a manner similar to their owners, and taken to the Bereavement Office for collection by relatives. The staff have a routine like anywhere else in the hospital, and are happy to help. They've helped us out frequently. Not just for cases of missing property, but for other police purposes. Part of a police officer's training involves becoming familiar with such things as having to see dead bodies, and so probationary officers often visit the mortuary as part of this routine. Having to see your first dead body can be a memorable experience. I remember some years ago one such new recruit was to be subjected to a cruel practical joke which most probably would not be tolerated today. A colleague climbed into one of the drawers and was planning to surprise the youngster when the mortuary technician pulled it open by sitting up, and appearing to come back from the dead. The prank, however, backfired on this officer pretty spectacularly. Even before he arrived at the mortuary another colleague, also in on the idea, had already climbed into one of the drawers with the assistance of the technician. A short time later, the mortuary technician then assisted the main prankster into the neighbouring drawer. Other colleagues then deliberately delayed their arrival, allowing the two officers, but mainly the second prankster, enough quality time to really absorb, to really get a feel, for their surroundings. Not to mention the cold. They sneaked into the mortuary in order to make sure they heard, and fully enjoyed, the next part. The second prankster was obviously lying in his chilled drawer, in total darkness, awaiting his opportunity to come alive when the drawer was opened at any moment. He naturally assumed he was surrounded by dead people. So it came as a huge, huge shock to him, when the body in the next drawer grabbed his arm and said:

"Christ, it's cold in here…!"

LOGISTICS

At the bottom of X-Ray corridor is South Corridor. This is where the Logistics department is based. Fortified like a cold-war nuclear shelter, and partly underground, it is where a good deal of the technology lands on campus. Infra-red detectors, heat detectors and thick steel bars everywhere; I doubt Fort Knox or the Bank of England are better protected. All IT equipment is property marked in several ways with the latest crime prevention ideas, and chemically etched with the hospital name and postcode. Anyone stealing these things has got to be pretty dense. But of course, so they are.

Logistics staff know when to expect deliveries of new equipment, and where on campus it will be located. Useful, inside information. Priceless to someone with betrayal and theft on their mind. Lap-top computers, being so ideally portable, have always been targeted by thieves. A number of lap-tops had been disappearing in regular, ubiquitous circumstances across the campus. It was around the time of Bobby Todd's activities, but not *all* could be laid at his door. The *modus operandi* was different anyway. Sometimes a lap-top would only be in situ on a desk for a day before it went missing. Sometimes it wouldn't even *reach* the department for which it was intended. Some were being stolen from secure offices, with no public access, and even overnight. Such mysterious circumstances surrounded the loss of ten or more lap-tops in a matter of a few weeks.

A breakthrough came when security rang me about something they'd found on the CCTV. One of the office buildings on the western fringes of the campus had no less than three lap-top computers stolen in one night. There was no sign of a break-in of any sort. One computer had been stolen from each of the three floors. This was either arrogance or stupidity. Or both. The CCTV revealed one of their own hospital security guards, on night shift, going into the building early one morning, then coming out a few minutes later, then back in, then back out again. What on earth was he up to? A security guard? Surely not? This particular guard, Anthony Miller, was not the most popular of the crew. I didn't know him very well as he mainly worked the night shifts, and my dealings with them were relatively few. But I did know him by name, and he knew me. He was a young, stout-looking chap with a round face and ruddy complexion. He had the beginnings of a 'Mr T' persona going on – despite not being black – as he had started wearing a quite flamboyant preponderance of heavy gold chains around his neck, and numerous chunky signet rings and sovereign rings, on his fingers.

Inside the building the internal CCTV had picked him up going over to where each computer had been stolen on each floor. He'd then made a pathetic, amateurish, and thankfully completely botched job of trying to destroy internal CCTV evidence, which left an even bigger trail to follow. To top it all, he was also recorded on the ID card swipe database too. He lived quite close to the back of the hospital on a notorious housing estate. So I paid him a visit, early one morning, with colleagues, warrant in hand. His buxom young girlfriend, snot-nosed baby in her arms, opened the door to us, before we could bash it in, and I immediately found a hospital lap-top, plugged in, in the corner of the lounge. Above the sound of the adverts on *GMTV* booming out from their television, which seemed to be so big it took up an entire wall of the living room, I managed to establish Anthony had already left for work at the hospital on one of his rare early morning daytime shifts. We searched the house, took the lap-top, and left. We went straight to the hospital security office. I asked Nigel, the security manager, to call Miller back to the office on his radio. A few minutes later he trudged into view, in his typically Neanderthal, indolent manner from North Road, and up the path towards the office. For an instant, I wasn't entirely sure of how to handle the situation. Miller had been on my side, on *our* side in the fight against crime. This was new to me. It almost felt like he was one of *us*. I've always been quite diffident in circumstances such as this, when breaking new ground, unjustifiably so, according to my line manager. So I decided to play it straight, by the book, and entirely professional, as the situation demanded. Standing at my van, I opened the cage. As Miller came up to me I slapped my speed-cuffs on him, pushed him into the cage, and said:

"You're nicked, pal."

I spent that day with my colleague, Gary, who'd assisted in my dealings with Bobby Todd. He needed the experience, bless him, as he was much more junior in service than I was. Once Miller was safely lodged in his cell, Gary and I went for breakfast at a cabin in the car park of a builders' merchants in town, rather than the hospital canteen. No other reason than it was nearer the custody suite. We'd started the habit of eating there when dealing with Todd. I ordered my usual, double egg cob, red sauce, cup of tea, no sugar. The order now tripped off my tongue like a favourite line of prose. Gary ordered his usual, the quite appropriately named 'fat bastard' special. Two eggs, two sausages, in fact two of everything you could think of, fried, in a massive white cob the size of a large dinner plate. Well, two dinner plates, actually. We sat side by side in the cab of the van, egg yolk dribbling from our cobs onto our uniforms. On more than one such occasion, while watching the many builders collect their materials opposite us, I would philosophise on my life, relative to the day's activities. That morning I made the comment, which inevitably invited a reply:

"I wish I'd been a builder."

"Why?" Gary said, idly, taking care not to bite his finger ends off, while holding the mother of all breakfast cobs.

"Because I'd actually *make* something, *build* something I could show people, and say 'I built that', instead of going around ruining people's lives, like I do now."

"What *are* you on about?" he said, looking at me, genuinely puzzled.

"This morning. Miller. I've destroyed his life. He'll be sacked, get a police record and probably never work again..."

There was a brief silence, broken only by the sound of a fork-lift truck we could see across the car park, and our two sets of jaws grinding and chewing like a couple of cows in a field. Gary just looked at me rather sternly. Then, with perfect timing, and in between huge mouthfuls of breakfast cob, some of which was escaping undetected out one corner of his mouth, replied:

"The thieving cunt deserved it, you daft old twat."

Here, here, Gary, well put.

We interviewed Miller after breakfast, after successfully wiping half of it from the front of our uniforms. I was convinced Miller had been assisted in conducting his thieving activities around the campus. He was as thick as a plank, so he must have had help. After applying a little gentle pressure, he gave us the name of his criminal associate. A chap who worked in logistics. Still keeping Miller in custody, we went in search of Mr Big.

Same procedure. John Webber was at work. In front of his colleagues, who just stood around watching in open-mouthed, blank astonishment, we nicked him, cuffed him and bundled him into the van. I can explain a little as to why television and Hollywood detectives often work in pairs. Real ones do too. It's the old 'good cop', 'bad cop' routine. It can actually work very well. It can also be hugely enjoyable. Gary and I developed this rapport between us when dealing with Bobby Todd, and it continued with Miller and Webber. It's not something which is pre-planned, you understand, it just tends to happen spontaneously while in interview. One of us becomes noticeably more emollient and sympathetic, while the other becomes very serious, almost aggressive. Human nature being what it is, when under significant pressure, and outnumbered, the subject will cling to anything, and anyone, he or she believes may be throwing them a life-line, however tenuous. Any tiny, remotely tender remark, therefore, thrown into such a situation can be like a baited hook to a fish, or life-vest in a choppy sea, when jammed in between some harsh questioning. Unusually, neither of these two had legal representation in interview. This does not mean a green light to rule-breaking. It is taped, after all. But I admit, it can make things a little easier. It certainly speeds up the process. Webber was under a lot of pressure.

Neither had been arrested before, but *he* was sweating. He was, of course, entirely clueless as to how we'd found out about him. He was unaware Miller was in custody. I could tell he was both very curious, and very scared. We told him some of what we knew, just to throw down a bit of corn. He then went on to tell us the rest. Their stories were identical. Webber completely immersed himself in a warm bath of confession.

So it was revealed the two of them had worked together for months stealing hospital lap-tops. Webber's part in it was two-fold. He would give Miller the tip-off as to when the deliveries were made, and subsequently where the computers were to be located. Miller would steal them, and pass them to Webber to clean up. Webber was a bit of an IT nerd, so could remove all of the inconvenient stuff from the hard drives, like patient records and so on. Miller couldn't do that, because, as I suspected, and as Webber stated in interview, Miller had no IT skills. Oh, and he was as thick as a plank too. Some of the computers were sold on. I found one in Miller's locker at work. Another at Webber's home address later that day.

Was this greed? Well, following the routine 'spit-test' (which is just what it sounds – and applies to all persons arrested for acquisitive crime) it seemed Webber had a very expensive cocaine habit. No wonder he was sweating. Eventually, much was made of the fact patient records were lost, in addition to the usual breach of trust aspect. Both were sacked and both given suspended prison sentences. Doesn't anyone go to prison these days?!

The 'Dugout'

THE FLASHING BLADE

Close to Logistics, off South Corridor, are the cancer wards. Next to them, endoscopy, and clinical haematology. It was in one of these busy departments 'The Flashing Blade' worked. I'd never met him before, and can't even recall seeing him around the campus prior to all this. But then, why should I? There are thousands of staff, so I'm not likely to meet them all. In the last few weeks leading up to Christmas, this particular year, there had been several vague reports of a 'flasher' seen on the campus. Whoever it was, if it was only one person, was amazingly omnipresent, as these sightings of him seemed to be all over the place. Also, if it was the same person, then this chap had a libido which he just could *not* keep down. He obviously wanted to proudly display his manhood to others, to make public his uncontrollable virility, regardless of whether they wanted to see it or not. 'If you've got it, flaunt it', as the saying goes. Up until Christmas, the reports were evidentially so nebulous in nature, that I didn't formally record any of them. Perhaps I should have, in hindsight. But experience sometimes showed this type of crime was rare, and the perpetrator did not usually strike in the same place over and over, like this chap. It generally stopped before the offender was caught. This was different.

I was lucky enough to be granted leave that particular Christmas, and I returned to work mid-way through the first week in January. I came back to find a large number of calls on my answer-phone, and emails from hospital security. The holiday period had been a busy time for the Flashing Blade. Christmas Eve and New Years' Day were particularly busy for him. There had also been some '999' calls from staff, by-passing security. When police had attended, there was never any sign of the offender. Though with some slight variations, a common description was beginning to form. The man was quite tall, dark, probably of Mediterranean origin, slim, with curly black hair down to his collar, under a brown baseball cap. His age ranged from mid twenties to late thirties. Not a massive amount to go on. He was always clean shaven, casually dressed, and didn't ever say anything. He would usually approach his victims stealthily, and only a few yards away from them he would then just go for it, right there, in front of them. The victims began to give accounts which were becoming more serious in nature, and evidentially much clearer, and consistent.

On my arrival at the security office that first cold January morning, Nigel and I started to check through the CCTV in the areas he'd been sighted. Security had already accumulated some useful material, some of which was from just the day before. It was time consuming and often tedious, but we were able to establish two principle areas of the campus where the majority of the incidents had occurred. In addition to this we began to find the same chap on CCTV walking towards the scenes, then a few minutes later walking back to where he had started from. We had a face, but no name. There had been some 'flashings' on the Bank Holidays, and in a way this made our job easier; there had only been a skeleton staff on duty on these days, and few members of the public, rather than the usual frenetic hustle and bustle in the main corridors.

This chap became relatively easy to follow around the campus.

Luck always seems to play a part in crime investigations. Maybe it's knowing when to recognise a piece of luck and take advantage of it which helps. While I was sitting in the security office that morning there was a report of a previous flashing victim having sighted the offender in North corridor. The victim had also then seen a security guard and quickly pointed the chap out as he apparently passed them both in the corridor. The guard radioed for assistance but in the meantime went up to the man and spoke to him. With typical professional arrogance the suspect said to Ricky, the security guard:

"You know me, I'm a doctor, I work here, I can't stop, I'm very busy, sorry..." and so on, and promptly walked off.

Ricky was alone, and frankly unsure of his powers at the time, so allowed him to leave. But he had the presence of mind to take a good look at him, and saw a hospital ID badge hanging around his neck on a blue lanyard. He noted down the name on a scrap of paper: Dr Alexander Mikos Younis, Registrar. By the time other guards arrived at the scene the doctor had gone. But we now knew who he was. A doctor!

There had been a dozen or more reports of indecent exposure in the previous six weeks or so which were probably this same offender. I made an assessment of each one and collated a list of complainants. Statement paper in hand, I toured the hospital seeking out witnesses. There were two main areas where the majority of incidents had occurred. The first was a secluded area, just outside, off North corridor near anaesthetics. The other was a similarly secluded area, also outside, near East Entrance, at the end of South corridor; just around the corner there was an alcove area, a recess between buildings, colloquially known by staff as 'the dug-out'. There were no windows over-looking either location. These areas were surveillance-free and used by staff in order to have a secretive cigarette. Smoking was banned on the campus, even in the open air. Staff, and patients, should in theory walk to the main entrances and literally stand off-campus, in the main road, to smoke. Understandably, some staff had neither the time nor inclination to comply by these rules, so these unofficial smoking areas were very popular. These were the areas targeted by the Flashing Blade. As a consequence, I initially found the witnesses quite reluctant to come forward. It was obvious they'd been contravening the hospital's no smoking policy. It was rumoured staff had been dismissed for such a relatively minor misdemeanour in the past when the policy was first introduced. I had to give them an assurance no action would be taken against them. It was obviously for the greater good of the hospital.

The first witness, and victim, was a young male nurse called Shane. A very amiable chap, he came across initially as quite a camp, Kenneth Williams type character. But Shane was far more astute and intelligent than any shallow, first impression of him may have shown. He had bright blue eyes, a radiant smile, and a lively exuberance which made taking a statement from him a real pleasure. He possessed a great sense of humour, matched by some brilliant observation skills, and so was an equally brilliant witness. Shane described how he'd been standing outside anaesthetics, on Boxing Day, alone, smoking a cigarette. He had a coffee in one hand, and cigarette in the other. There was a large, sporty motorcycle chained to the foot of a steel fire escape some twenty feet from him. He often dreamt of owning such a machine, but somehow knew it would never happen. He didn't even drive a car, or possess a licence, for that matter! The door to North corridor was behind him and past the motorbike the gap between buildings led to the end of a service road. Shane noticed a man standing next to the motorcycle. He was a tall, dark, Spanish or Greek-looking chap with black curly hair protruding from under a brown baseball cap. The man was also smoking a cigarette. Occasionally he would glance in Shane's direction, while taking long pulls on his cigarette. Shane paid him little attention, as he didn't appear particularly friendly, and he was certainly not his type anyway, so he said, and not a good looking man at all. He'd had a very busy morning, and had been on duty since seven. He was tired, hungry, and still a little hungover from the night before. It *was* Christmas, after all! He stared idly up at the clear blue December sky, contemplating finishing work at five o'clock. Then he noticed the chap was no longer standing at the motorcycle but was a lot closer, at the corner edge of a building only a few feet away. He seemed to be staring at Shane intently, not taking his eyes off him. Then to his disbelief and utter shock, Shane could see the man's right arm moving rhythmically, slowly at first, under his clothing. There was the beginning of a smile appearing across his face as his arm movement began picking up pace, faster and faster. Shane stated he did not directly see the man's penis, as it was obscured by part of his coat, but there was absolutely no doubt what was happening. He was close to the door into North corridor, so he opened it quickly and went inside, leaving the man there. Both Shane and I found this very disturbing. But more was to follow.

When thinking of 'flashing', the perception is of a type of harmless, comical, Dick Emery or Benny Hill character who would run up, open his rain coat shouting "Hey look at this!" before quickly running away, laughing. In reality, however, as in this case, the true-life experience is far more disturbing than comical.

I managed to trace two female witnesses who'd been victims while enjoying a cigarette in the 'dugout' near South East Entrance. Near this entrance is one of the biggest car parks on the campus, suitably named East car park. There are some good cameras covering this area, and inside the entrance itself. But no camera covers the dugout, and the opening is obscured from view by shrubs and bushes. The size of a small room, there are four steps down to a lower level, past a gap three feet wide at the entrance, adjacent to a waist-high wall. Someone had placed a couple of plastic chairs in there, and the ground was inevitably littered with cigarette ends. Sandra and Carol, both nurses, had been sitting in the back of the dugout for a few minutes, smoking, and engrossed in their own conversation, mainly about work. They had coffee with them, and it was near lunch time. They both noticed a man appear at the entrance to the dugout, smoking. He had positioned himself at right-angles to them, leaning on the end of the wall, but by so doing, had effectively blocked their exit. This fact did occur to Sandra at the time, but then the thought faded from her mind like a passing shadow.

The man was standing slightly above them, in silhouette. Carol didn't even notice at first, as she was far too busy updating Sandra about a particularly awkward patient she'd been dealing with earlier. She was facing Sandra too, not directly at the entrance, and the man.

Sandra nudged Carol with an elbow, once, then again. She discreetly leaned her head as though trying to point at the man. No opaque fumbling about this time. The man was standing only a few feet away from them, staring to his front, at the wall. His erect penis was sticking out, plainly, and hugely, from his zipper. He had it grasped in his right hand and was masturbating calmly and steadily while the two women watched on. Both Sandra and Carol were understandably very shocked, and suddenly became very fearful. Their distress was amplified by the fact they were trapped in there, with him blocking the entrance. Once Carol saw what was happening, she became by far the better witness. She described in clinical detail, perhaps how only a nurse could, the man's precise actions. His hand moved faster and faster while his facial expression remained unchanged. There was a very slight sound of his arm moving rhythmically against his coat, other than that there was complete silence, there in the dugout, between the three of them. After a few brief minutes, which they stated seemed far, far, longer, the movement suddenly stopped. He was seen to finally ejaculate directly into his hands. Carol was sure of this. It was an indication of the proximity in which the man was standing, that this was so clearly visible. Then without saying a word, or even looking at them, he appeared to wipe his hands with a tissue, or handkerchief he took from his pocket, put his penis back into his trousers, zipped up, and hurried out of sight. I wondered if he'd been thinking forensically by not leaving anything at the scene. Though professionally Carol and Sandra deal with patients on a most intimate, personal basis daily in their nursing work, this incident was still a huge shock to them. I assumed he would wash his hands before returning to work and having further contact with patients!

My thoughts, and those of my colleagues, were that if this man was capable of such behaviour as this, what else would he be willing to do? What was his next step? Criminals do tend to take their offending up another level in most circumstances. How much would it take, given the right circumstances and opportunity, for him to get physical with one of these victims? He was not a small chap, at least six feet tall, and reasonably well built. Quite capable of over-powering a lone female. We had to put a stop to his coffee-break activities sooner, rather than later.

I gathered all the evidence I had and drove to his home address with my usual posse of willing helpers. When he answered his front door, Dr Younis was very polite. He was well-spoken, co-operative and obliging. His English was superb, despite the fact he was of Greek and Egyptian origin. He had a generally calm, relaxed demeanour. But he was having none of it. He told us in his ultra-polite manner, that we had the wrong man. He had legal representation from the outset and had very lengthy consultations with his solicitor. He was utterly refuting all the allegations made against him. He had a lot to lose, so this was perhaps to be expected. I played all the hospital CCTV to him, which showed him walking towards the scene on several occasions. He was seen walking towards the dugout, past the cameras on South corridor, past South entrance, and on to East. As he walked he could be seen changing his clothes on the move. He had a bag on his back from which he took his brown baseball cap and a coat, then put the bag back on his back. The bag, the cap, and the coat, were all on the CCTV, identical to the ones described by the witnesses. He was seen walking back from each scene a few minutes after each incident. He walked back along the same corridors, stuffing his flashing outfit back into his bag. We found this whole outfit hanging up in his hallway at his home address, and I produced them as exhibits. I knew we had the right man. I suspected he realised how much evidence we had too. But he remained rock solid behind his denials.

Most of his replies to questions were 'No comment'. As I touched on earlier, I had huge maps of the campus prepared by staff in the Facilities building. One of the hospital architects, Glen, assisted me in pacing and timing the various possible routes he took from his office to both scenes. With a map of the hospital, the two of us walked from the doctor's office to anaesthetics, then to the 'dugout' and back to his office. Glen had a measuring wheel and we must have appeared rather strange, the two of us, me in full uniform, pushing this thing around the campus. Up and down stairs, along the corridors, in and out of the doors and back again. We had very accurate timings and these routes were printed electronically in different colours onto the maps. These timings coincided exactly with his ID swipe card readings, from leaving his office and returning. But he was challenging everything.

One morning, I agreed to accompany the doctor and his defence team, which consisted of a smart-looking, middle-aged male solicitor and a rather corpulent young woman with a note pad, who was almost constantly scribbling away, even while walking around the campus to the relevant areas. Nathan, a young security guard, walked around the campus with me, while the doctor and his small entourage visited the 'dugout' and paced the corridors, stop-watch in hand, muttering furtively to one another as they went. The woman was drawing diagrams on her pad, as far as I could tell, labelling them with arrows and numbers. I tried to catch occasional glimpses of what she was doing, but she kept it annoyingly close to her body, aware of my casual but keen glances, as though teasing me with it. Nathan had a greater knowledge than I of the various doors the doctor could have used, and we made sure we pointed out all the possible escape routes he could have taken. He did not use East entrance, as it has a very good overt camera on it, so he must have used one of the permanently insecure side doors when accessing the 'dugout'. I remember button holing his solicitor and pointing out one of these doors, even showing him how it opened, just around the corner from the 'dugout'. He looked at his client in anticipation of a reply, but the doctor just said, as calm as ever:

"I've never used that door, never"

Nathan started to say out loud precisely what I was thinking, calling into question the doctor's honesty, but there was little point in an argument. That would wait until the trial. When it was time to charge him I'd taken over fifty witness statements, and had dozens of documentary exhibits, from the huge maps, to the many CCTV discs. I charged him with three offences of indecent exposure. Two in the dugout and one outside anaesthetics. It finally went all the way to Crown Court.

We lost the case. Well, we didn't lose it exactly. The judge would not proceed with it, on the very first morning of the trial. He stated the identification evidence was 'unsafe'. I knew why. So did the prosecuting barrister. Very early on in the enquiry, one of the security guards, over-keen, but in genuine ignorance, had taken the doctor's photo from the ID database and shown it around some of the witnesses. These were, by coincidence, the same witnesses who had successfully picked him out in an electronic ID parade later, known as a 'VIPER'. This therefore compromised and contaminated the identification evidence. I knew this had happened, and made no secret of it. But the judge stated it was of such importance that without it, there was insufficient evidence to proceed. We appealed for hours that morning, but to no avail.

I assisted in the hospital's own internal discipline hearing. The Flashing Blade was dismissed. Their level of required evidence is similar to that of a civil court and is a 'balance of probabilities', rather than 'beyond reasonable doubt'. So the only punishment which befell him was the sack. He appealed, but the decision, thankfully, was upheld.

By the way, there are a few things I've so far not mentioned about this chap. Shortly after his arrest his head of department rang me, concerned about what had been found in his office drawers. He had three large drawers in his desk. Each one was tightly packed with pornography. But it wasn't simply a few adult magazines, though there were plenty of these. There were also hundreds of A4 pages, each one in a clear plastic sleeve, with things stuck on each side. On each page someone – presumably the doctor – had stuck pictures of bras and panties, and close-up colour photos of female genitalia, which had been painstakingly and meticulously cut out from catalogues and porn magazines. This was clearly obsessive and disturbing. I had mentioned this to the prosecutors early on, but they seemed surprisingly uninterested.

The other thing was, and more importantly, he'd been caught masturbating in public before. Twice before, in fact. And arrested on both occasions. The latest occasion was in my own city only a year before. He'd taken out his erect penis at a lone female in an isolated bus stop late at night, not far from the hospital.

SOUTH

It was May. I'd had another call from a ward manager on South Corridor: Elizabeth McCarthy. I'd not met her before. She wanted to see me about 'some thefts in the department', but wouldn't elaborate on the phone. I'd been at work since 7.50am and had just finished my cereal. I always found it far too early to eat at home before work on this shift, so took milk in a small bottle, cereal in a bowl and ate at my desk while checking emails. I also checked the intelligence briefing database, and a similar one which logged calls to the police in the area. This was vital in order to know what had been happening overnight, or when last on duty. By 9am I was ready for the outside world. I'd finished my cereal and drank two cups of tea. I washed my cereal bowl in the kitchen, exchanged pleasantries with the cleaning staff and caretakers, and took it downstairs to the locker room. I collected the rest of my kit and went back up to my desk. It's not actually *my* desk, but a desk I use when on duty. It's in a communal office in the uniform section of the station, overlooking the main road. On the wall above the computer I keep photos of all my local 'nominals', as we call them, persons who have been in trouble and who I need to constantly monitor. There seems to be more and more every year. Most of them are young males, under thirty. Of all the problem lads I try to keep an eye on, every one of them, I mean ALL of them, are from what used to be described as a 'broken home'. They live in a house where there is no adult male, or father-figure of any sort in their lives. Usually, but not always, a workless household. But then, though entirely true, these are not currently politically correct observations!

I picked up my utility belt and buckled it up around my waist. It has hanging from it along its length a heavy ASP collapsible steel baton, rigid speed cuffs, first aid kit, Velcro leg restraints, pen-knife and document pouch. Then I put on my 'stab vest', which is also apparently good for stopping certain kinds of bullets. But not those from an M16 or AK47, as these fly about at far too high a velocity. I suppose I'll just have to take my chances then! My stab vest has pockets which I utilise very well. I keep my pocket book, which has the size and appearance of one of those nineteen-eighties 'filofax' folders, in the left side. In the right I keep a panic alarm and a small pair of binoculars. Also quite a large bunch of keys to the local community centre. I'm an honorary key-holder. My radio hangs from the outside of my stab vest. All together the belt and the vest, with contents described above, weighs fifteen pounds. I carry a certain amount of essential paperwork around with me too, such as statement paper and blank interview paper, folded over in half. I file this down my front, between the stab vest and my shirt.

The weather was awful, despite it being springtime, so I donned my bright yellow fluorescent jacket. I grabbed my lid and black leather gloves, and walked through the nick to the front door. I walked out of the double doors, and down the steps into the pouring rain. To be blunt, the modern uniform is useless against bad weather. Rain drips off the equipment straight onto your legs, soaking them through in minutes. In the old days we had trench coats which reached down beyond the knees with high collars.

Brilliant. I remember one winter standing between a row of terraced houses at three in the morning, completely covered in snow from head to foot. A man suddenly walked into the alley where I was standing and almost died of fright. Those were the days when we used to patrol on foot on night shifts. At the traffic lights I crossed, as usual, without pressing the pelican lights. If you know how the traffic behaves, and the phasing of the lights, you can time it just right without having to cause unnecessary delays to drivers. I know these lights very well. Maybe I just like the additional risk involved too. I can always tell when the rain is heavy and prolonged, when I am in it, as opposed to slight and intermittent. In heavy rain, drops of water start to accumulate on the end of the front peak of my helmet, right in my vision. The droplets channel themselves along the shallow 'v' shape along the sides, and then drop off the end, and onto my coat or, more usually, my legs. This will happen quite quickly in heavy rain, within a few minutes in fact. In fog or drizzle, it may take hours of exposure to the elements.

It's about a half mile to the hospital. Not far in good weather, but seemingly much further in a heavy downpour. I bolted undercover at the first opportunity, via North East Entrance. Along North and left down X-Ray onto South. I seem to have been very busy on South Corridor. Perhaps it's due to the sheer number of wards, and the comparatively high number of patients and staff working in them. I walked up two flights of stairs to the doors of McDonald ward. The doors were locked. I took my hospital ID badge from its holder, hanging from my stab-vest, and swiped the card reader. The magnetic door lock clicked, and the small LED light on the reader changed from red to green. I really do enjoy using this card. I enjoy sneaking around all the 'Restricted – Staff Only' areas, in full uniform, unannounced, and without having to knock or otherwise beg permission to enter. I suppose it's good of the hospital authorities to allow me this privilege, as it certainly is. So I enthusiastically make full use of it. I pulled at the door and it opened heavily. Inside the ward on the immediate right were the ward manager's offices. Elizabeth, or Liz, as she liked to be called, and as it was printed on her ID badge, was on the phone. I tapped on the door, which was propped open, and walked in. I stood just inside her warm office when Liz saw me over her shoulder and finished her conversation. I was dripping all over the floor. Small pools of water gathered at my feet. A number of droplets landed on some patients' notes, so I decided I must take off my helmet and coat and sit down before I caused any more damage. I also unhitched my belt and dropped it to the floor. It landed with a loud percussion of steel and leather onto the carpet tiles. I took off my stab vest and piled it all up in an untidy heap near the door. I thought I may well be there a while anyway, judging by the nature of the call and from previous experience with Cheryl Bawtry. I wasn't wrong.

Hospitals are full to bursting with sick people. This is an obvious fact. But oncology, in my humble opinion, is different. A huge proportion of the patients here are not just sick, they are dying. Not only this, they may well know they are dying too. If you've had a stroke, a chest infection, or a broken leg, the prognosis is usually one of recovery, surrounded by lots of up-beat positivity. Cancer wards are mostly bleak places, shrouded in a winter mist of dark, saddening, and cruel inevitability. I can only just imagine working in an environment such as this, day in, day out. I often thought the working life of a police officer was pretty dismal at times, but this must be far worse. I have nothing but admiration for the staff in these circumstances. Except the tiny minority of thieving staff.

Liz began to tell me of mysterious disappearances in the ward, and her office, of various items ranging from hospital property and colleagues' property, to gifts and donations from the public. She'd often accused her partner at home of taking small amounts of money from her purse, as did other colleagues with their partners. It seemed so many members of staff had money stolen from their bags and purses it was virtually endemic across the whole department. But no-one was ever sure just how much, when and where their money went missing. There seemed to be a repeat of Cheryl Bawtry's MO, but even more widespread and indiscriminate. I recounted the Bawtry case to Liz and she was obviously very shocked. But I noticed while telling her about Bawtry, Liz nodded frequently, almost knowingly, as though it was all quite familiar to her. She then began to give me strong hints as to who the offender may be in this case. The thief could not be a visitor, or a patient. Neither last that long. The thefts had been happening for months. Their cleaning staff were very long standing, well known, and trusted. The offender must, therefore, be someone *ab intra*, a member of their own ward staff.

Just for a moment I imagined the long road ahead of me. All the statements, the frequent visits to the ward, enquiries with staff and patients, and the time involved digging this thief out from under their cover. He or she must be hunted down and caught. I had to send in the beaters to thrash about at the dead bracken and undergrowth, to disturb them and force them out to face the guns. I had no evidence of any sort to implicate anyone. I needed to set a trap. I knew from experience the thief would not stop, but would become more and more daring and greedy. Despite probably seeing me on the ward, and maybe even speaking to me, the offender would not be able to resist what I'm sure they considered to be easy pickings. There was absolutely no indication, after all, that they were not able to continue their predatory habits. Liz and I worked together on a plan, of sorts, to set traps for the thief. Items were placed in Liz's office, and she kept a detailed account of when and where the next items were stolen. I asked Liz to record exactly who was on duty when things disappeared, even the smallest items. Hopefully a picture would emerge that may lead to enough circumstantial evidence to make an arrest. One step at a time, in no rush, we hoped we would be able to accumulate what we needed.

That was May. I heard nothing from Liz until September. She rang me again and asked me to visit the ward. There was the beginning of an autumnal chill in the air when I walked to the hospital that day, and I thought just how quickly that year had passed. Liz was pleased to see me and shut the door behind me.

"I think I know who it is." She said, in a quietly excited voice.

"Who?" I replied, surprised, even a little shocked, but nonetheless keen to hear the reply.

"One of our auxiliaries."

Liz passed me five sheets of paper on which she'd written brief details of an incident at the top, as a title, such as 'Margaret's £20 note' with a date, and a list of more than a dozen or so names underneath. On each page all but one of the names were crossed through. There was a name common to each incident. This same name was on each page, in varying places on each list, and had not been crossed out: Amelia Philomena Johnson. Five thefts had been listed. Margaret, a nurse, had £20 stolen from her purse. Another colleague had £5 stolen. Another £10 . A bottle of perfume, an obscure brand I'd never heard of, in a particular blue bottle, called 'Merle' had been stolen from Angie's desk. Finally, but worst of all, £180 cash had been taken from Liz's filing cabinet. This was money donated by grieving relatives. Liz had been so upset by this particular theft , she'd replaced the bulk of it with her own money. I took out my statement paper and listed the thefts in date order. The sheets of paper became a police exhibit.

The following few weeks saw a bonanza for our thief, who became particularly greedy. Two young lady doctors in the department were targeted. One had her phone and purse stolen, the other a debit card and cash. The same debit card was used later that afternoon in a cheap 'pound shop' in a nearby town. Coincidentally the same town Amelia Johnson lived in. I drove up there and luckily the very helpful staff had retained the sales invoice which also became a police exhibit. It was one of very few retail outlets which still relied entirely on a signature, and not the more secure 'chip and pin'. Obviously why it was used by Johnson. If indeed it was Johnson. There was still nothing particularly convincing. I needed a little more, just to be sure. Just to eradicate any doubt. The answer came late one Saturday night.

The ward was almost fully occupied, but very quiet. One two-bed area of the ward was occupied by a mother and daughter. Jackie Seely was thirty-two, slim, with shoulder length black hair, freckles, and pale blue eyes.

She had been in the ward for the last eleven weeks. Her mother, Joan, was sleeping in a makeshift bed next to her, on the floor. There was another patient in the room, but was out of sight and sub-divided off by a ceiling-to-floor curtain. This other patient was extremely ill, and completely bed-bound. It was around midnight that Jackie requested a bath. Her mother helped her out of bed and into her wheelchair. As they left the room to travel the short distance down the corridor to the bathroom, a nurse was particularly over-attentive to them. She insisted on making their beds despite protestations from both Jackie and Joan that it was entirely unnecessary. So they finally relinquished, and left her fussing around their beds. An hour later they returned and slept peacefully through the night. This was the only time they had left their bedsides, and their bags. At eight in the morning they went together to the nearest coffee shop and noticed, with a deep, desperately sickening feeling, as they later described, that they had been victims of crime. How could this possibly be? In a safe place such as a hospital? They counted and re-counted their money but the result was always the same. Jackie had a hundred pounds missing from her purse. Her mother, Joan, had thirty pounds missing. They began to look accusingly at everyone and anyone around them. They retraced their movements since the time they were sure they last had their money. Their thoughts then turned to the fussing nurse. It was Amelia Johnson. Apart from Johnson there had only been two other members of staff on duty that night. The other two were fully registered, experienced, and long-serving nurses. Johnson was a jobbing nurse, not a regular career nurse like the others.

I attended the ward early the following Monday morning. I took statements from Jackie and Joan. I found that the statements from both women were evidentially brilliant and pretty straight forward. Apart from Jackie's. I'd already written 'I am very ill at the moment but hope to make a full recovery'. Further down the same page it occurred to me to be a little more specific as to the nature and seriousness of Jackie's illness, partly to demonstrate the callousness of the thief. I tried asking her exactly why she was a patient in this ward and had been for so long. How does anyone ask with any subtlety this particular question in an oncology ward? Seeing me obviously struggling, Jackie suddenly looked at me with her pale blue eyes, straight into mine. She then issued a very gentle sigh, almost like a soft breeze, and said to me, quietly, but with unambiguous clarity:

"My cancer's terminal..."

I looked down and hid myself in the statement paper. Had I been able to, I would have probably pulled it over my head. I then wrote exactly what she'd just said. I did not cross out my own feeble, earlier assessment. I had absolutely no words available to me to make any sort of verbal reply. I felt as though for that instant, sitting by this hospital bed, I'd forgotten every single word I'd ever known in the English language. My hand-writing deteriorated as I finished the statement. At the end, while she was signing each page, I said to her:

"Can I just say I think you are very brave..."

I know this probably reads as being a rather pathetic thing to say, but I really did mean it. This relatively young person, with a child of her own at home, knew she was soon to die, but could still sit talking to me about it, as apparently calm as she was. I could see, however, that she was now becoming a little lachrymose, as I admit I was. I think we both recognised this in each other, briefly, so we both quickly changed the subject. I shook her hand, said goodbye, and went outside to speak to the staff. Four nurses were standing quietly around the reception desk looking, unusually, as though they had no work to do.

"I didn't know her illness was terminal. Is this true?"

I said, hopelessly naïve, and looking at them all briefly in turn. After a moment, one of them replied, matter-of-factly:

"Yes. She's not curative." Yes, she's going to die, in other words, I thought.

I spoke to Liz. Johnson was off duty that day. Due back on at seven the next morning. I'd had enough. Time to bag this bastard. Gary was available, I knew that much. I recruited the assistance of a female colleague too, Stephanie. We were 'go' for 5.30a.m. the next morning.

That night, as with most such nights preceding such a 'raid', I woke up several times before the alarm clock. A mixture of excitement and nervous anticipation . It could only go two ways. She would collapse and readily admit her guilt, as with Dr Chu, or she would say, and admit, nothing. We pulled the large police van up outside her end terraced house at exactly six a.m. I walked up to the front door, which was actually down a short driveway, and through a pair of high, open, wrought-iron gates at the side of the house. As I knocked on the door it was opened by Johnson herself. She was fully dressed, ready to leave for work. I realised then that I'd seen her in the ward before, as she had me. Nevertheless I introduced myself and she invited us into the kitchen. I then remembered I'd actually spoken to her several times, months before, in the ward, when initially investigating the thefts. It occurred to me then that she had the opportunity to stop her thieving and think herself lucky, but had obviously ignored the warning signs. In order to take advantage of the power to search on arrest, the suspect had to be placed formally under arrest. They must also understand exactly what they are being arrested for. There were potentially so many thefts I suspected her of, that I simply said to her:

"Amelia, you are under arrest on suspicion of numerous thefts in the oncology department this year".

It then became clear as to what her initial reaction was going to be. She very calmly said in reply:

"What thefts? What do you mean? I haven't taken anything."

I started searching the kitchen. These were some of the most untidy people I had ever encountered. Every single cupboard was literally jam-packed with stuff. Packets of food, tins, boxes, sweets, drinks cartons, all crammed into each cupboard so they were filled to bursting. And I had to take it all out, one item at a time, search each item and each cupboard, and put it all back as closely as I'd found it. Gary and Steph went upstairs. After an hour I'd found nothing. I was three-quarters of the way around the kitchen, nearing the sink. One cupboard left. Amelia was sitting at the dining table in the open-plan area adjacent to the kitchen. I would guess she was probably feeling pretty smug at that time. Her conversation was light, unconcerned and irrelevant. Then Gary appeared from upstairs:

"I found these in the wardrobe in the main bedroom." He said, handing me a large black handbag, some purses, a blue bottle of 'Merle' perfume and an expensive mobile phone.

There was a neat, thick wedge of twenty pound notes in one of the purses. The other purse contained store cards. None of the names on these store cards were Johnson.

I took out the police headed note paper entitled 'Contemporaneous Search Record', which had been unused up until then, and began filling it in. I held up the first store card, in the name of Emily Philips, and I asked Johnson:

"Whose is this?" as I fixed a very serious stare at her from across the room. She didn't reply. I said again: "Amelia, whose is this, where did it come from?"

Again silence. But then she started crying. She flushed deep red.

"It's a patient's. I took it from a dead patient."

In common with some other thieves I've dealt with, she collapsed into a blubbering mess. More from the shock of being caught than any genuine remorse. The game was up: She was caught. Like a rabbit in the headlights. She had no explanation other than the truth. I held up six cards in all. She admitted stealing them from various dead or dying patients in the oncology department. I noted down each reply. She signed the notes. I'd not heard of any of the names on these cards. Further victims I didn't know about who would need to be traced. Or at least their relatives and next of kin. She admitted the 'Merle' perfume was from Liz's office and the phone belonged to one of the doctors. As the investigating officer all this was such good news. I felt like screaming from the rooftops! At the very least I knew I'd be getting a charge for the theft of these cards, the perfume and the phone. I then asked her about the money. It looked to me to be over a thousand pounds. At first she stated it was all hers. Savings for a family trip to Florida. I asked her to sign to this effect. Then as she did do, she stated some of it was stolen. In fact, all of it was.

I continued my search of the kitchen. I'd obviously unwittingly saved the best until last. I found hospital equipment, obviously stolen, stuffed in the back of the cupboard behind pots, pans, and packets of food. She admitted it all belonged to the hospital and she did not have any permission to remove it. Stolen, then, in other words.

I filled in the search record and when we'd finished there were thirty five exhibits. Stolen items. We left the house at eight o'clock, two hours after our arrival, with all the exhibits in brown paper bags, and Amelia hunched over in the cage at the back of the van, like a recent unwanted donation to a primate zoo. Back at the station I interviewed her slowly and methodically. I enjoyed it. The memories of my encounters and conversations with the distraught victims, and their next-of-kin, were still very prominent in my mind. I asked her about each item in turn. She admitted some, and denied others. She made up some stories and she openly admitted some thieving. As I've said before, it's virtually impossible to deny evidence found in the home of the accused. She admitted a good proportion of things put to her. Seventeen in all. She admitted fraudulently using the doctor's debit card in the pound shop, several times actually, not just the once. She admitted stealing Liz's charity money too, and she stated she knew it was from public donations. She admitted specifically targeting patients who were in their last minutes of life, or had just passed away, in order to steal from them. In the trauma and grief that followed, next of kin either chose not to report items missing, or were too upset to do so.

When it came to submitting the case to the Crown Prosecution Service for a charging decision in the usual way, I was shocked with the reply. I suspected I would be instructed to charge two or three of the best offences and

'TIC' the rest. This was the usual manner of disposal for so many offences of a similar nature. A small sample of the worst were usually charged, the others simply ' Taken Into Consideration' and thereby attracted no separate penalty. The reply in this case, however, was to charge eleven offences. In the eyes of the CPS, Johnson had obviously behaved in a particularly despicable and nefarious manner. The other six admitted offences could not be charged, as the aggrieved were now dead and next of kin untraceable. In fact I had some difficulty chasing around the city for the victims, with some urgency. A total of eight had died during the course of the enquiry. This obviously constituted much of the nefariousness of the crimes, no doubt. I very much regret to say, with some sadness, before Johnson was finally dealt with at court, Jackie Seely had also passed away, at home. She had asked her mum to pass on a message to me, near the end. It was simply:

'Thanks for your help.'

DECOY

It *is* a shock to deal with thieves such as Amelia Johnson, and the other members of staff tempted into dishonesty at the hospital who I've had dealings with. None – other than the Flashing Blade – had ever been arrested before. All must therefore have passed the various screening tests and criminal record checks at interview and recruitment stages. This does not preclude criminal behaviour though, quite obviously. Certainly many have been employed for years, and personal circumstances can change. Particularly financial circumstances . But it must be remembered there are *thousands* of staff working at this hospital, with dozens of wards and departments. The campus is a village community in itself, or even a small town, during the average working weekday. There are bound to be thieves, therefore, among such a community, as in any other. I am a thief catcher, amongst other things, and it is my job to apprehend them and take them before the court. I am an evidence-gatherer, not judge and jury. So I catch these people when I can, and go about my business every day the same.

The wards on the south side of South Corridor face some substantial greenery. A cricket pitch complete with ramshackle pavilion and a line of tall poplar trees adjacent to a deep, steep-sided brook. The hospital side of this brook has a sloping grass bank, while on the other side there's a high, very formidable and totally inaccessible wall. The brook marks the boundary between hospital land and a strip of green owned by the city council. Then there's a main road. A line of trees and bushes obscure the brook from the hospital. Between this line of trees and the brook is a gap just wide enough in which to drive a car, should anyone want to. I did, once. Unusually one afternoon I was in a marked police vehicle, a very old diesel Vauxhall Astra, which was hardly ever used. It sounded, and drove, like a very old tractor. If it did start up, clouds of thick grey-black smoke proffered out of the back in huge billowing clouds of soot, with an accompanying, and very loud *clack clack clack* from the engine. The POLICE livery was peeling off all over, and it had faded terribly. None of the young cops ever drove it. They hated it, and called it 'The Nail'. I loved it. It was probably twenty years old, and I could well remember when I drove such cars as a young officer on 'Response' duties. I sometimes employed this old thing as a decoy, and left it on the campus occasionally when auto-crime was a problem. This tactic seemed to work pretty well, that is until it was sadly vandalised and totally destroyed by fire one night on a nearby housing estate.

Anyway, I was about to place it in a particular car park for the night and was touring the campus with one of the security managers in the front passenger seat. We were assessing which was the best location in which to leave the old police car all weekend. A call came through Mark's hospital radio that two lads were acting suspiciously in the bottom of South car park, near the brook. The blue light on the roof didn't work, neither did the siren (in fact, I don't think it even *had* a siren!), but I doubt I would have used them anyway. We were too near, so no need for dramatics. I drove the police car up the kerb onto the grass near the cricket pitch and between some boulders, which had been put there in order to deter travellers from using the site. I drove around the edge of the cricket pitch and quite miraculously managed to avoid some trees. The car then lurched through some tall grass and up close to the side of the brook. Ahead of us I could see two figures, a couple of hundred yards in front. The car was coping well with its challenging bit of 'off road' driving; in fact the poor old thing seemed to be relishing the excitement, probably as much as I did. We then managed to get safely onto the grass strip between the trees and the brook. Halfway along this dead-straight quarter-mile, narrow length of grassland, the two lads turned and saw us. I suspect that they did not imagine we would pursue them in the car. Not there. I guessed this as they calmly turned back and continued walking towards the end, and the edge of the campus, with their backs to us. How dare they ignore us?!

I dropped the gears down one and depressed the accelerator, gently at first. The grass was probably damp, but I could feel the drive wheels were providing a suitable amount of grip, so pressed the accelerator harder still. There was no barrier to our right, nothing to prevent a vehicle from traversing irretrievably into the brook, probably ten feet down a muddy grass bank and into three feet of water. Probably because it wasn't *meant* to be driven on! Up into second, then into third. The lads turned suddenly, hearing the Astra's clacking diesel approaching. I admit the adrenaline was at a considerable level by this time. This was a failure on my part. Police drivers are supposed to drive professionally and dispassionately at all times. This is entirely so that you don't beat the living crap out the suspects if and when you eventually reach your destination. As the old car began to pick up speed, I wasn't sure what was going through Mark's mind, not until well after the event, anyway. Having no siren or blue lights I decided I had to make some alternative, additional noise as we drew ever closer onto the heels of these two running reprobates. So I wound my window down and stuck my head fully out of the side of the car. Of course this then gave me a much closer look at the brook down below to my right, and exactly how close the wheels of the car were to the edge. By now travelling at over thirty miles an hour, on a strip of land just a little wider than the vehicle itself, with trees on one side and a deep ditch on the other, I let out a shriek which seemed to me highly instinctive at the time, and very appropriate to the occasion. I screamed:

"Yeeeee-haaaah!!!" as loud as I could, followed by several "Come back here, boy!!!" in wild-west style rebel yelps.

Did I think I was in an episode of 'Dukes of Hazard'? Mark must have thought I'd gone completely and utterly mad. I wasn't thinking at all, really. I had no idea what I would have done if the lads had stopped running. As far as I was aware, they hadn't even done anything wrong. It would have been too late anyway, as by that time they were only a few yards in front of me. If they'd fallen, or otherwise come to a stop, I'd probably have run them over. They must have been absolutely terrified. Who was that nut-case in the old police car screaming out of the window? Luckily they reached the end just in time, and ran up the grass banking, through a gap in the bright blue steel railings, and away. They didn't look back once. I managed to stop the car at the end, safely, turned left and drove it gently through a hedge, and into the far end of South car park, between some rocks. No damage done. I don't remember Mark saying anything in the car. But later, over a coffee, he told me in great detail, with the help of some very colourful old Anglo-Saxon expletives exactly what he thought. It was some years before we had prowlers on that car park again. The next day the caretaker of the cricket pavilion rang me and reported what he assumed were quad bike tracks around the pitch:

"Fucking vandals..." he said to me.

BUMP

Up from the cricket pitch at the western end of South Road, the area is populated by numerous large, mature horse chestnut trees. Conker trees. In spring they are a beautiful sight when in full blossom. The many cone-shaped bunches of small, creamy-white flowers covering the trees are reminiscent of Christmas decorations. In the autumn the ground around them is rich with an abundance of conkers, most of which are left unseen, untouched, and wasted, like discarded treasure. Some of these conkers really are enormous. Round, ripe, and shiny, like samples of polished teak or rosewood, these many arboreal jewels invite you to pick them up just to touch and admire them. How quickly the seasons seem to pass when walking amongst them again. Close to these trees is a new car park where another of the old red-brick buildings stood until recently. I dealt with a non-stop road traffic collision there not long ago.

No longer called road traffic 'accidents', as the word 'accident' implies a blameless incident beyond anyone's control. In reality there's almost always blame, of course. A member of staff returned to her brand new car one very hot afternoon in June to find the rear of her vehicle completely bashed in. The back bumper bar was all smashed , the rear of the car was badly dented and the impact had caused the car to be moved forward about six feet from where she'd left it. It looked for all the world like it had been hit by a madman driving a truck. The damage was later estimated at nearly two thousand pounds. Naturally, she rang security immediately, who in turn rang me. With so many thousands of vehicle movements a day on the campus, this is not uncommon. Thankfully, in most cases the drivers resolve the problem amicably between themselves, in an honest and civilised manner. But not always. As in this case. So I plodded my way down to the hospital and swiped my way into the security office. On a warm day, even in shirt sleeves, the 'stab vest' is hot and uncomfortable. So much so it just has to be accepted. An inevitable aspect of wearing it. At least it's only thirty degrees, I thought to myself, and not the suffocating forty or forty-five degrees as in some other parts of the world. I always wear a cotton t-shirt under my uniform shirt. Even in summer. After only a short time, both are so wet with sweat on a very hot day, they could easily benefit greatly from being pushed through a mangle. I still prefer this to being cold though.

I sat with Nigel and we scanned the CCTV from the two cameras covering the new car park. We found a car, an old Nissan Micra, being driven into the car park, just around lunchtime. The driver didn't seem to know where he or she was going – we couldn't see the driver's face – and seemed to drive into the car park quite hesitantly. They held up traffic on South Road briefly while obviously wondering whether or not to use the car park in the first place. In fact it was a staff car park and not open to the public. Anyway, the car was driven in and stopped between two rows of parked cars. The driver then promptly selected reverse and drove back, hard, into a car parked in the line. The Micra hit the back of the parked car with such force it moved it back with a violent thump. Clearly it must have made quite an audible bang as well as a perceptible jolt inside both vehicles. The offending vehicle was then driven out of the car park and away, at precisely 1.30pm. The driver didn't stop, get out, leave a note or anything. Amazingly, on the CCTV the Micra did not immediately look like anything had happened to it as it was being driven out of the car park. Maybe it would fall to bits around the corner?

We had all this on a clear, colour, digital moving image, saved onto a hard drive, and now on a disc. I remember thinking how beautiful the trees looked, as some branches waved and jostled their way into the picture on a gentle summer breeze. I imagined what the countryside outside the city would look like on such a beautiful day. I imagined what the *French* countryside would be like on such a clear, cloudless summer day. I thought of the Luberon hills and wondered if they were sunny that day too. I could almost hear the cicadas, and smell the lavender. I thought how very hot it was, and how sweaty I was in my uniform. I could feel a droplet of sweat slowly tracing its way down one of my legs in my trousers, and how my damp clothes were sticking to my back. I stood up, and left Nigel in the security office. I had the disc and some CCTV stills clearly showing the car being driven in, the moment of impact, and then out, only a minute or so later. It was registered to a female living only a mile or so away. So I walked down to see her, armed with my stills. I walked in the shady sides of the streets, in order to avoid melting any further. As I approached her address, in a tree-lined, quiet street , of neat ,semi-detached houses, I saw the car outside the house. I was looking at the front of the vehicle and so walked around the back expecting it to be as badly damaged as the other car. Not a scratch. Not a dent or a mark anywhere. At least, I couldn't see anything matching damage associated with hitting the other car the way it did. I at least expected the back bumper bar to have fallen off, or *something*. The Micra was very old, and had a slightly worn and weary appearance anyway. But I was astonished the back was not completely crumpled up, and couldn't believe what I saw. This was only the *next day*. How could this be possible?

I knocked on the door and a woman around my age answered. I quickly established the owner and driver was her mother. She led me into the house and out the back onto a small but very pleasant patio area. This was a very nice house, in a very nice middle-class area. The registered keeper was sitting at a green wrought iron cafe table, the days' papers spread out before her, with what looked like tea in a bone china cup and saucer. She had bi-focal spectacles around her neck on red and blue coloured string. It was later in the afternoon, and seemed even hotter. There was a tall, quite resplendent, turquoise-blue wisteria climbing the wall near the back door, a few feet way. It's scent was strong, almost overpowering, but at the same time sweet, and delectable. I removed my helmet and could feel my hair was soaked, sticking to my head. I stood there before them utterly drenched in perspiration. She was seventy-nine years of age. Quite small and petite , with a very pleasant smile. I was offered a cup of tea but declined. I thought I wouldn't, seeing as I might be about to report someone for driving offences. It appeared they'd just had lunch. There were two small gold-edged plates on the table with remnants of breadcrumbs and crusts dotted around. On reflection, I now know I was utterly beguiled by the situation. The pleasant, middle-class , afternoon tea atmosphere, and the lady herself. She was softly spoken, and seemed incapable of being dishonest. In fact I thought myself to be rather rude and presumptuous even thinking this lovely old lady could be my 'hit and run' driver. I heard myself apologising for intruding, and tentatively sat down at the table with them both. It looked and felt like a country scene from an old black-and-white British 'Miss Marple' film. I almost stood up and left without even making any enquiries, or asking any questions, chastising myself for the intrusion. But I had to do *something*, at the very least. I took out my pocket book, and pen. The sun was in my eyes and I suddenly felt at a distinct disadvantage.

"Is that your car outside?" I said, trying to assert some professionalism.

"The Micra? Yes, yes it is. Why?"

I hesitated, and probably even coughed, stereotypically, but knew I was obliged to say what I said next:

"In that case I have to caution you, as I have reasonable grounds to suspect you may have committed an offence relating to the use of the vehicle."

I issued her with the formal thirty-seven word caution and she looked a little surprised but remarkably unconcerned.

"Oh dear, officer, what's this about..?"

"Did you drive into the hospital grounds yesterday at all?"

"Yes, yes I did."

"What time?"

She turned to her daughter and they briefly talked about what they had for lunch the day before, then the word 'appointment' came up.

"My appointment was two o'clock. But I couldn't find anywhere to park."

"Did you drive into one of the car parks, at around

lunchtime, then drive straight out again?" I asked, rather sheepishly, still bemused by the fact the vehicle wasn't a total wreck.

"Yes, I did. I think so. Why?"

"Well, because your vehicle is on CCTV reversing into another, in a hospital car park. You must have known about this?"

"Me, no, it couldn't have been me. I went to the hospital, but I didn't hit another car…"

"At about one-thirty yesterday lunchtime?"

"Yes, that would be about right, yes."

I showed her the stills. Though quite graphic, they would not show the other vehicle being pushed along several feet by the impact. She looked straight at me and denied any knowledge.

"But this is clearly your car, is it not?" I pleaded.

"Yes, yes it looks like my car."

"Then it was you, and your car, which hit the other one."

"No. I don't remember hitting anything."

I was exasperated. It was obviously her, but she wouldn't admit it. Or maybe she really didn't know she'd hit the other car? Maybe she was mad? I couldn't shout at her or make veiled threats, not to a little old lady. She signed my pocket book interview notes and I left. I took another look at the Micra. There was no visible damage to the vehicle.

I had the disc copied. I sent one copy to the aggrieved, and one to the little old lady. A formal warning in a letter accompanied the disc to the old lady. It advised her to be more aware of her driving in future, and in particular when conducting manoeuvres in car parks. The CCTV, along with my notes, was conclusive. I considered the offence of failing to stop and report the accident. But this was impossible. The car park was a restricted area not open to the public, and therefore exempt from such offences under road traffic law. But, the victim was happy. I heard nothing more for months until I was contacted by the victim's insurance company. It seemed the little old lady was still denying the collision took place, even though she admitted to me at least, it was she who drove the car in the car park at the material time. I thought the matter had been resolved long ago. I was very surprised by this and rang the other party's insurance company. I told the chap from the insurance company to contact the old lady's insurance and to ask them to ask her about the disc I'd sent her. The old lady's insurance company eventually rang me themselves. 'What disc?' the chap said. 'The one I sent her showing the accident clearly.' The chap had no idea the disc existed. She had not told them about it at all, or even anything of my input into the incident. I advised him to ask her about it. Little old lady indeed!

I spoke to our 'Vehicle Examiners' about the collision. An older Nissan Micra could indeed cause a considerable amount of damage to a new car with modern 'crumple zones' at the back. That's what they are designed to do. The older cars are more rigid in construction and may appear undamaged on the outside. But they could have some serious and dangerous chassis damage underneath. So, even a little old lady in a little old Micra can inflict a lot of damage. It doesn't have to be a madman in a truck. In this case, on the face of it, neither the car, nor the driver, were telling me absolutely everything!

JIMMY

From this car park there's a steep climb. Up a supposedly 'restricted' road towards Out-patients, then Maternity further on. At the bottom of the hill are some tall, white, oxygen storage tanks, behind a sturdy chain-link fence. Areas of these are crusted with masses of thick ice, even in summer. A hundred yards up, at the top of the hill on the right, is a semi-derelict chapel. This hill is therefore known colloquially as 'Chapel Hill'. The small church, as it once was, has been closed for as long as I've known it. One of the few remaining old red-brick buildings, also no doubt due for demolition. On the left is a small chimney sticking anonymously out of the ground, set in a block of concrete, just by the road. Steam issues from this chimney almost constantly. On several occasions distressed members of the public have run up to me, hysterical, claiming there's a car on fire at the top of the hill. At the western end of the campus there are more trees. Tall oak and ash mix with aging chestnuts, more numerous around the old buildings. Outside the Outpatients block I made an arrest one afternoon some years ago. A particularly obnoxious young man who just would not, or could not, understand normal civilized behaviour. Jimmy Ellis was twenty-four and a local lad. Like most of my arrests on campus I'd been wanting to speak to him for a while, but so far he had evaded my attention. The previous week he'd been on campus, the day before, and again earlier that same day. He'd been rude and abusive to staff, and they wanted me to at least speak to him about it. I didn't fully realise the extent of his obnoxiousness until the day I arrested him. He had a very young daughter who needed regular dialysis, three times a week. His partner was of a similar ilk to him, and virtually feral in her attitude and behaviour.

I had a call from staff in the unit asking for police assistance. By the time I arrived, Jimmy had gone. The nursing sister had contacted me out of sheer desperation and fear. The baby had been attending the unit for several weeks and was by all accounts making good progress. But until a kidney donor could be found, as – presumably – in most of these cases, the poor little thing would have to be on dialysis for years to come. But I never did see the baby, the subject of everyone's attention, not in any kind of calm, relaxed manner anyway. The baby should have been the centre of everyone's attention. Or so it should have been. Maybe the father, Jimmy, was feeling a little put out by all the attention his daughter was receiving and his fragile ego could not cope. Anyway, his behaviour had been gradually deteriorating at each visit. On this particular day I happened to be on campus and spoke to the staff about the latest incident. He'd been rude and abusive, of course, but this time it was worse. Far worse. Two female members of staff had been reduced to tears. A male doctor was frantically typing a do-it-yourself letter on a computer, banning him from further visits to the ward. Something really had shaken them this time. I asked Jane, the ward sister, what had happened. She told me that about thirty minutes after their arrival at the ward, once the baby had been safely established onto dialysis, Ellis took it upon himself to actively seek out members of staff in order to terrorise them. There was really no other accurate way to describe his behaviour. Firstly he

approached the male doctor who had successfully put the
baby onto the dialysis that day. He stood an inch from the
doctors' face and shouted, apparently so loud it silenced
the whole ward:

"Fuckin' sort my fuckin' daughter out you fuckin'
wanker..! If you don't I'm gonna fuckin' kill you, you
fuckin' cunt!"

Spittle was flying at the doctor's face, and he was so
close he could smell the stale tobacco and alcohol on Ellis'
breath. He could see black streaks on his yellow teeth, as
he ranted and raved obscenities. The doctor tried to back
away with every expletive, but Ellis made ground on him
equalling every step as he did so. Apparently there had
been a small drop in some progress reading on the baby's
chart, nothing serious or life-threatening, and probably
not helped by passive smoking in the home, but Ellis
wanted the world to know just how upset he was. A
female nurse interjected and was then also subjected to a
ruthless tirade of vile abuse and threats. The nurse was so
frightened she stood with her back to a wall in the ward
while Ellis went up to her, as close as he could get without
touching her, fists clenched, screaming in her face:

"You, you fuckin' cunt, you fuckin' sort 'er out an' all.
Get her fuckin' sorted out now, or I'll fuckin' smack you,
you fuckin' cunt!"

He ranted like this for what seemed several long
minutes but was probably only a minute or two. Another
female nurse went to her colleague's aid and was subjected
to the same treatment. She burst into tears. Despite twenty
years of service, it was too much: Not something faced
every day in a quiet children's dialysis ward. There were
pictures of smiling faces on the walls and teddy bears
everywhere. These all seemed remote and redundant to

the staff in these terrifying few minutes. After rounding on the ward manager, Jane, Ellis left, slamming the doors and screaming abuse as he did so. He was accompanied by an older male, who was apparently his father. *His* parenting skills were obviously not quite up to standard either, as he did nothing to reign in his son's behaviour. Other patients and visitors on the ward sat completely aghast at what they had just witnessed. It was then that Jane rang me. This was the atmosphere which greeted me when I arrived, only a few minutes later.

I quickly took some statements from the staff directly threatened by Ellis. Just enough, in case I managed to apprehend him. Then I went to see his partner. Kylie was sitting by the baby in a private room while the dialysis was going on. The small bundle that was the baby was lying still in the bed, and the machine she was connected to was quietly whirring away, doing its job. After introducing myself I said to Kylie:

"What's wrong with Jimmy. Why is he behaving like this?"

"Like what? What the fuck you on about? What's it got to do with your lot anyway? What you fuckin' doin' 'ere?"

I tried to explain the boundaries of civilized behaviour but found Kylie was clearly not in the least bit interested and began talking over me. So I raised my voice. As she did. So I did. Eventually I won, as I could shout the loudest. She started crying. Among several F's and personal insults from Kylie, I finally managed to glean they were both worried, and tired, from having a child as sick as theirs, with all the encumbrances associated with it. This was obviously the reason for Ellis' behaviour. After so long in the police, I have reached a level of understanding regarding people such as this. They have no rational way of calmly expressing their feelings like normal people. Very often the only way they feel able to express themselves is through shouting abuse, threats, and then the next level, physical violence; among themselves and towards others. I believe we were rapidly approaching the final threat level. Ellis needed to be nicked or we would soon have some injured hospital staff on our hands. I left Kylie and the baby and stood in the corridor outside. I needed a quick search of the campus, preferably in a vehicle. I shouted Gary on my radio, who luckily arrived a few minutes later in a small police van. We drove slowly around the campus. I knew Ellis was still around, with his father, so it was just a case of finding him. We were looking for a chap in his twenties, with an older man. It was, as I said, outside Outpatients that we found them:

"Mr Ellis?" I said, as I got out of the passenger side of the van.

"Yeah? So what? What do you lot fuckin' want?" he replied, in typical form.

He was taller than I had imagined, from the description given to me by the ward staff. Several inches over six feet. But thin, and scruffy, like a lot of these types. He was unshaven and had mousy-brown short hair, which was greasy and lying flat on his head like an old nylon rug. Though not a particularly cold day, he was wearing a very thick coat, padded like a life-vest. This, combined with his height, caused him to look reasonably tough, probably well beyond his actual weight and frame. Little wonder he was able to cause so much fear in the hospital staff.

"I'd like to ask you some questions, would you sit in the van a minute please?"

"What for? I've done fuck all."

"Yes, but just have a seat a minute while I have a word with you please."

I pulled at the side sliding door of the van, and he climbed in. By this time Gary was also standing outside the van. Gary is a man of not insubstantial physical presence. I doubt Ellis would have been so astonishingly co-operative had he not been there. Ellis' dad was commenting on how innocent he believed his son to be, and just how unreasonable Gary and I were. He expressed his displeasure and a dislike of police officers generally. Suffice to say he didn't say it in this manner, but in his own opprobrious vernacular, so had to be warned about his language. But other than that he didn't get in the way at all. It must have come as no surprise, at least to him, that the ward staff had contacted the police. I leaned in the van and quickly slammed my speed-cuffs on Ellis' right wrist. As I did so, I said to him:

"You're nicked. Threatening behaviour."

I cautioned him as I managed to get the other cuff on his left wrist. I tightened them up. He shrieked and shouted abuse... I twisted them, ever so slightly. He shrieked and threatened me again.

"Stop swearing please," I said to him, calmly, and gave the cuffs another very slight, imperceptible twist, to which Ellis reacted immediately by letting out a shrill, high-pitched shriek of pain. I'm sure most of this was probably fake. This almost always happens in these circumstances. Potentially violent 'hard' men, when restrained with hand cuffs, invariably start to moan and even cry about how much the cuffs hurt, like some mardy little schoolboy. Their very tough character seemingly disappears immediately. Perhaps this is the true nature of all bullies. Of all the equipment I carry around I've used my cuffs far more than anything else. The relatively new 'rigid' cuffs, also known as 'speed-cuffs', are just brilliant. Even if you can get just *one* cuff on the person, you've effectively won, and have control. With two, one on each wrist, they'll do anything. Really. With both cuffs on correctly, that is, between the base of the hand and the wrist knuckle-bone, even the very smallest twist can cause the most excruciating pain in the subject. This is not outwardly visible to onlookers either, as the movement is virtually undetectable, which is even better.

I lifted Ellis out from the back seat of the van and opened up the rear doors. Leading him by the cuffs, in order to maintain complete compliance, I put him in the cage and slammed the door. Gary drove us back to the nick, leaving the dad standing outside Outpatients, muttering insults, looking suitably blank and fumbling with his cigarettes.

It was only a five minute drive back to the station from there. Ellis continued shouting abuse and insults. Really nasty, disgusting, foul, personal abuse. I then understood first hand exactly what the staff in the dialysis ward had been through. I didn't even get the full picture, however, as Ellis was safely cuffed and locked in the cage at the back of the van. I could only imagine what it felt like an inch from my face. I then launched into my own mini-tirade, aimed at Ellis. I felt I needed to point something out to this man. He needed to know some burning issues, things which were already on my mind, but which he came to crystallize, right there in the van.

"Right. Shut up now." I shouted. He initially ignored me. So I tried again:

"For fuck's sake, shut up! Shut up and listen to me!!"

I shouted, as loud as I could. This time I had his attention.

"What do you think you are doing, shouting abuse and threatening hospital staff?! What's going through your tiny fucking mind when you are threatening the very people who are trying to look after you and your baby?! Are you completely and utterly fucking mad?! You don't go around treating people like that! You need these people! You should be fucking ashamed of yourself! Look at you. You're just a useless fucking chav! No good to anyone! It's people like you who are destroying this country! You fucking sit around all day watching fucking Trisha expecting everyone else to sort your fucking lives out for you! Well it doesn't fucking work like that you arrogant fucking shit! Are you listening, you fucking bastard?!"

I'd shouted this as loud as I possibly could, in his direction. I wasn't proud of it. Far from it. I'd lost it. I'd lost my temper and it was unforgivable. Very unprofessional. I'd shouted so much my voice started to fail on me and my throat became painfully dry and uncomfortable. I found it exhausting and wondered how anyone could maintain such an aggressive mental attitude without making themselves ill. But from the back of the van there was complete silence. We drew up to the station gates and still silence from the cage. The gates opened and we drove slowly into the station yard. Then a faint noise which surprised both Gary and I drifted out from the back of the vehicle. Ellis was sobbing. He was *really* sobbing. Snot was beginning to pour from his nose and the tears ran uncontrollably down his reddening face.

"I'm sorry, man. I'm sorry. Yeah, I know. Shit. I'm sorry. I'm sorry…"

We arrived at the nick and opened the van. Ellis was surprisingly polite from then on. He was all 'please' and 'thank you'. His language and manners were impeccable. The model detainee.

Gary had a good laugh at my expense later. But he'd seen me in this effusive state before. Ellis admitted threatening behaviour and was charged and bailed to keep out of the hospital campus. He was served with a notice by the hospital authorities banning him from the hospital. They can do that you know. It took a few weeks, but Kylie and the baby were moved to an alternative hospital, quite some miles away. Ellis went to court and was fined and given some minor order or other as 'punishment'. He should really have spent a few months in prison, so he could thoroughly reflect on his behaviour.

A few months later I had an email from a police officer in a neighbouring force, but some distance away. I was being asked for my opinion of Jimmy Ellis. I wondered how he knew of him. Then it clicked. His partner and daughter were using the outpatients' dialysis department of their hospital. On visiting days, apparently, Ellis was going around the ward being abusive and threatening the staff…

SOUTH CORRIDOR

IRISH PETE

In an ideal world, the hospital, as big as it is, would be my entire beat area. There is certainly enough for me to do, as you have been reading, at the hospital. But sadly this is not the case. In fact, despite its size, and the amount of work I have at the hospital, it forms roughly one third of the beat I have the responsibility to manage. The other two-thirds are a council estate of social housing and a middle class estate of privately-owned, detached houses. Need I have to inform you, the middle class estate of mainly professionals and relatively wealthy retired people rarely see me. But I do try to show my face as often as I can. My time is therefore divided mainly between the council estate and the hospital. Sometimes these two areas can overlap, as in the case of Irish Pete. I visited him at his flat once every few months or so, and for the last few years saw him occasionally at the hospital, frequently hanging around outside Outpatients at the top of 'chapel hill', smoking. He lived in a small block of flats at the bottom end of the council estate. He was a regular out-patient at the hospital. Latterly a more frequent patient due to his illness. He had throat cancer. So I saw him at both locations. But I'd known him for years. I believe in the old style of policing, whereby the local cop walks a beat, and stops occasionally to chat to locals, getting to know them, and them likewise getting to know him. This type of policing really works and can pay huge dividends. The public love it too. The criminals don't care for it though. But that's because it works. People develop a trust in you, and they start to tell you things. Frequently I will stop and chat to residents on the council estate or even get invited in for coffee. They will spend up to an hour or so telling me all the local 'gossip' on the estate. But of course a good proportion of this is not 'gossip' at all, but intelligence. I walk away trying desperately to remember it all and, when at a safe distance, reach for my pocket book and write it all down. Information imparted to me with the words, 'But I'm not a grass...' No, of course not.

Irish Pete never really told me anything worth calling 'intelligence'. Plenty of gossip, rumour, speculation and scandal. Who's seeing who in the flats, whose dog is a bloody nuisance, who's just moved in next door, who's moved out and so on. I suspect the first time he invited me into his ground floor flat was in order to avoid being seen talking to a uniformed police officer at the door. That combined with a good deal of genuine Celtic hospitality. I don't remember the first time I was invited in, but it was years ago. I was probably making some enquiries into some nearby crime and hoped he may have heard or seen something. I remember being told by another resident of the flats 'Go and ask Irish Pete, he might know.' He invited me in, anyway. I often wondered how I would keep a small flat, on my own, devoid of any feminine touches of any sort. It may be similar to the way Pete kept his flat. Very neat, very tidy, but not particularly clean. I suppose if it was my flat I would do some dusting when there was dust visible and not before. This was obviously Pete's philosophy too. It would be unfair to have described his flat as spartan, but it was definitely not cluttered. The long, straight entrance hallway led past the bathroom, single bedroom and into the living area. To the right was the open-plan kitchen, adjacent to which was a round wooden dining table and four chairs. This is where Pete sat. This is where he lived, in fact, when not in hospital. At this table. He sat with his back to the wall, facing the kitchen. He had a clear view of his small, ancient television at the other end of his lounge area. Equally important to Pete, though, was the view he had from the window. From there he could see most of the movements across the grassy courtyard of the flats. He always saw me long before I saw him. His net curtains made sure of that.

Pete was seventy-two years of age. Thinning grey hair combed back over the top of his head, which probably once resembled a 'teddy-boy' style. He had typically Irish blue eyes and a fresh-faced, slightly unshaven, but not altogether scruffy appearance. He was slightly built, quite thin and only around five foot six in height. He always wore braces and not a belt on his trousers. There was a profusion of rugs and mats on the floor of his flat. Rugs on top of rugs in a lot of places, in common with some more mature citizens such as himself. If you didn't sit down at his dining table when instructed to do so, Pete would be deeply offended. He was very insistent! So I usually sat opposite him, with my back to the kitchen, next to the window. When he heard doors bang shut, and voices outside, he could tell you immediately who it was and what they were doing, with complete unstinting accuracy. I was suitably impressed by this, but then realised just how many endless hours it must have taken to acquire this level of apparently fortuitous knowledge.

I took off my helmet and placed it on the table and put my black leather gloves inside. I unfastened my coat and pulled at some of the velcro holding the stab-vest around my waist. I was usually there at least half an hour, so I may as well make myself a little comfortable. I always accepted a cup of tea from Pete, as he was almost as insistent I drank with him as he was about sitting with him. I sat holding my mug of tea, listening to his latest gossip, hoping for something resembling real intelligence this time. He placed his tea on a coaster made of a square of newspaper, folded neatly to shape. Faded, stained and curling at the edges, it must have soon been time to make a new one. A tabloid newspaper lay open on the table, so he closed it and folded it up, with slow deliberate movements. It had been open at the crossword. He enjoyed his crosswords. There was a tin of tobacco, a cheap plastic cigarette lighter and an ash tray on the table, obviously stolen from a pub somewhere, but nothing else. I looked around the room and there was already a thick smog of cigarette smoke hanging completely still in the air in the middle of the lounge area. The walls and ceiling were off-white, almost yellow. The wall adjacent to, and above the radiator, next to the sofa was noticeably more streaked with a deeper yellow, where the rising warm air had concentrated the smoke.

On my last visit to his flat Pete was seated at his usual place at the table. Even though it was only ten in the morning, it wasn't tea he was drinking, but beer. The can was placed neatly next to his glass, and he took gentle sips from it, in between short, thoughtful pulls on his cigarette. My uniform and my hair, in fact everything smelt of cigarette smoke when I'd been to see Pete. He spoke with clear succinctness, describing his days in his softly curved Irish accent. I established on my previous visits that he was originally from a small cathedral town in the west of Ireland, on the border of County Mayo and County

Roscommon, called Ballaghaderreen. But despite still having a noticeable accent, he'd been in England for decades. Most of his adult life, in fact. Curiously, he'd never once been back to Ireland. I found this particularly strange. I'd asked him about this, but he would never elaborate. He'd simply shrug and say :

'Oh, well, you know, one o' dem tings, like...'

As he would when talking about his son, who also lived in England, but whom he never saw. He had grandchildren too, apparently, but as far as I knew, he'd never seen them. I found this incredibly sad. I always endeavoured to keep any conversation light, but I was curious as to how he filled his days. He watched television a lot, but was also surprisingly selective in his viewing. The television section of his newspaper was open on one of my visits and he'd drawn swirling, cloud-like circles over most of the listed programmes with his biro. I asked him about this. He just said:

"That's the stuff I *won't* be watching. Most of it's shite..."

Quite right too, I thought. He had strong opinions about almost everything. Terry Wogan, for instance, was 'not much of an Irishman' according to Pete. He was apparently now 'too English'. He spoke wistfully of his youth in Ireland, and I knew talk of this sometimes seemed to upset him, so I avoided it. He knew most of the other residents around him in the flats. He'd fallen out with his immediate neighbour and had refused to look after his dog for a week while the chap went in hospital.

"He's after getting himself one of those scooter tings off de social. But I saw the daft old cunt run like fuck for a bus the other day... I'm telling you, there's nothin' wrong with him at all..!"

I saw occasional glimpses of mischievousness and self-deprecation, as he once recalled when he'd had a new phone:

"I was watching de telly and the phone on de telly was ringing and ringing. I thought to meself, 'Why doesn't the eejet answer the damned ting?' – until I realised it was me own fuckin' phone that was ringing!"

He laughed out loud for a few seconds before this came to an abrupt and obviously very painful stop, with some deep, withering coughs.

Pete rolled another cigarette. Barely a few minutes after the other one had finished. His hands were shaking. I noticed he had quite long finger-nails, which were clean, apart from the index finger of his right hand, almost the full length of which was a rich mustard yellow, even deep into the wrinkles of his skin. He lit the cigarette and took a sip of his beer. He looked thinner than ever and not as clean as usual. His shirt was crumpled and there were great rings of stained yellow circles, like tide marks, under his arms. The centres of these were thick and crusty, multi-layered and cracked around the edges. He'd rung me the day before and left a message stating he wanted to see me. He then told me to forget about it, but I insisted he tell me. Eventually he revealed he'd given a teenage lad, apparently unknown to him, some money the day before to run to the shops for him, but the lad had not come back. It was not a lot of money, but he had no-one else to talk to about it, so he rang me. He didn't want to report it as a crime, as he stated he now felt very foolish. He then told me what I suspected was the real reason for my visit.

His throat cancer, in remission for the last twelve months, had returned. It was more aggressive than ever. Both sides of his neck and face were swollen. He complained of an acute dryness in his mouth, despite it clearly not being dry at all. He was to be readmitted into the oncology wards as an inpatient in a few weeks, where I had visited him several times the previous year. There was a selection of new underwear, socks, and a shirt, still sealed in their packets, on a lounge chair. These were ready for the inevitable day.

I'd bumped into Pete at the hospital, around the time he'd last been given the 'all clear'. He was in a buoyant mood, understandably so. But now it was back. I gave him all the usual platitudes given the circumstances. As I had done the year before. But this time it seemed different. He was speaking in a manner which was more despondent and sullen than I'd heard him speak before. I urged him to make contact with his son, but he stated he wouldn't. I gave him some frankly hollow reassurances and noted down his next inpatient appointment at the hospital. I would call on him when next patrolling South corridor. No inconvenience to me, as I would be passing anyway. It was likely I would be his only visitor, too.

I walked out of his flat, exhausted, into the fresh air outside. I never saw Irish Pete again. No-one knew, of course, to ring me when he died. I only found out when I called in to the oncology ward off South corridor three weeks later, the date of his appointment. He'd already gone. Apparently in the last few days the hospital had managed to contact his son, John, who had been with him when he passed away. I was glad he'd finally made contact.

SYMPATHY

I do sometimes see other residents of the housing estates at the hospital. They are only across the road, so this is no surprise. Very occasionally some of the youngsters from the council estate begin to congregate in the grounds of the hospital, as a new place to socialise, and cause the security staff problems by goading them and generally taking the mickey. They know the security staff are quite obviously not police officers and they make sure they tell them so. No-one would mind young people hanging around the hospital campus if they behaved. But invariably they don't. The cricket nets are constantly damaged and graffiti starts appearing everywhere. So they have to be told they cannot hang around on the campus. I can usually deal with this type of problem quite quickly. Security simply print off some of the photos of the youngsters involved, and most of the time I do know them. I take the CCTV stills to their various parents, or step-parents, and job done. They find somewhere else to 'play', after a stern warning from me.

I see one particular young person who lives on the council estate quite often when I walk through the estate. He's unemployed at the moment, thanks to me. Well, thanks to his own activities, really I suppose. Dave Kaye was nineteen when I dealt with him. He was a cleaner in some of the offices at the hospital, mainly on the South and West side of the campus, near the Outpatients block. He had a strict routine of cleaning only a limited number of these offices, at regular times. He wasn't very ambitious in his thieving, but he was persistent. Security had passed my phone number to the doctor in charge of this particular unit, Dr Rafiq, as the staff were becoming exasperated at the sheer number of minor thefts in their offices. The building was secure and not open to the public at all. For several months the staff reported to Dr Rafiq that anything they left out on their desks would disappear. This ranged from biscuits to pens, and from loose change to at least one mobile phone. When I first spoke to Dr Rafiq he was quite despondent about the problem and appeared to see no solution to it. I'd not met him before, or ever been in his department. After I'd introduced myself I was surprised to find out he had no idea the hospital had its own police officer. He was more than surprised to hear from me quite how much thieving there had been in other departments. He seemed reassured, and a little relieved, to hear his department was therefore not the only one in this situation.

Thinking of the other cases of thieving such as this, I started to ask the usual questions. It became clear very quickly what was happening, and who the offender may be. Dr Rafiq stated as far as he knew, nothing 'disappeared' during the daytime hours, when everyone was at their desks. This was understandable, as a thief may feel vulnerable if others were around, possibly watching. He stated the staff had now begun to lock their drawers at night after finishing work, and were not leaving anything on their desks at weekends. The thieving seemed to be reduced as a result. But the day before, a collection tin for someone's birthday was stolen, having been left out overnight on a desk. Probably twenty pounds was missing. The premises were locked up, usually by Dr Rafiq himself, at six o'clock every night, as everyone had usually gone home at around five-thirty. No-one worked there at weekends. The public could not gain access, so this was someone with keys and a lawful reason for entering the building. A security guard? A cleaner perhaps?

I left Dr Rafiq with my contact details, and a better frame of mind than when I'd arrived, and went to see Nigel in security. I needed to know if the premises were part of the security officers' patrol remit. They were not. As Dr Rafiq had stated, he, and his other staff on occasions, locked the building themselves at night. The alarm was set when the building was locked. Security never went in the building at all. I found the answer, as in other cases, with the ID card swipe system. Dave Kaye had swiped himself into the building at six-thirty the night before, to clean the offices. The night the collection tin went missing. He'd swiped back out at seven-thirty. No-one else had been in the building until staff arrived at eight the next morning to find the tin missing.

I went to Dave's house. His father answered the door. A polite enough chap, he told me Dave was out. I left him a note, asking Dave to ring me. This was late afternoon. An hour or so later Dave rang me. I asked him to come to the station to see me. This method of causing a suspect to attend the police station voluntarily is known as 'warning in'. A person is 'warned' in to the station. It is an alternative to arrest at work, at home, or even in the street. It was commonly used years ago, but nowadays not used quite as much. People invariably just don't turn up. I don't think the police are as respected as they once used to be! I was aware I could potentially lose evidence. But the only fully identifiable stolen item was a mobile phone, and the owner was unsure as to even the make of the phone, let alone any serial numbers. So I was prepared to give this option a try.

I remember I was sitting in the 'night kitchen' watching the news, eating my sandwiches at around five o'clock, when the front counter staff contacted me. Dave was at the enquiry counter asking to see me. Brilliant, I thought. I initially had suspicions he wouldn't turn up, but here he was. I'd not met him before and so I shook hands with him when I saw him. I ushered him into one of the interview rooms at the front of the station and sat him down. He was roughly the same age as my eldest son and not unlike him in some ways. He was six feet tall and quite well built, with messy, collar length hair, which is apparently quite the trend. He had a warm smile and an ingratiating, polite manner. He was very friendly and seemed to be in possession of an innocent, boyish charm. I knew straight away I wasn't about to arrest him. I quickly made a reassessment and decided to deal with him by an alternative, more lenient method. I left him seated in the interview room and walked down the corridor to the stationery drawers. I took out some 'contemporaneous notes' paper and returned to the interview room.

I cautioned him. I asked him if he wanted legal advice. He declined the offer of a free solicitor. I wrote all this down on the notes. Then I wrote a question down, before reading it to him, and came straight to the point:

"Dave, I know you clean in Dr Rafiq's building, at the hospital. You are the only person going in there at night. I can prove this. I know you were in there last night. I also know you took the tin with the money in it last night. Why did you take it?"

Of course I didn't know for sure that he'd taken the tin, but he didn't know that I didn't know. I looked him straight in the eye. With little hesitation, Dave then replied:

"I had no bus fare. I needed money for bus fare."

I was surprised and elated with the reply. A full and frank admission! But then, at the same time, looking at Dave, I heard a tiny voice of conscience at the back of my mind wanting to tell him to be careful what he said to me. Having dealt with career criminals who wouldn't know how to lie straight in bed, this was just far too easy. But I carried on:

"Where was the tin?"

"On a desk. I just took it."

"Did you take some biscuits?"

"Yes. I was hungry. I hadn't had any tea."

"Did you ever take a pen from a desk?"

"Yeah. I needed a pen, so I took it. I took a few."

"Did you take a phone?"

"No. I've got a phone. I don't need another."

"Did you take anything else?"

"I took some chocolate. There was always chocolate and biscuits lying around. I was always hungry. I took a few coins off a desk a few times too, but it wasn't much."

"But Dave, these things were not yours to take were they?"

"No. But... I just took 'em."

I wasn't sure about the mobile phone. He probably did take it. I asked him several times about it, but he denied taking it. I asked another couple of pages of questions, then he signed the notes, as I did. He was a nice lad who had just admitted a series of thefts to a police officer. He'd spent the money, eaten the biscuits and chocolate, and lost the pens he'd taken. He'd been very stupid. The only item which had a crime number attached to it was the collection tin. I wrote out an 'Adult Caution' form, right there and then. Dave had no previous convictions of any sort. I shunted him down the stairs to the custody suite and his DNA, photograph and fingerprints were taken. He was automatically allocated a PNCID, and a police record was thereby created. The custody sergeant issued him with the Caution. That was it.

I know for a fact that had Dave insisted on a solicitor being present, judging by the evidence available, the legal advice would have been to say 'no comment' to all my questions. Had this been the case, Dave would almost certainly have got away with it. The CPS would never have pursued it, the evidence was just not strong enough. This is just how these things can sometimes happen. But, he *was* stealing. He *was* betraying a position of trust, and so he *had* to be dealt with. It was my job. And I did it. This does *not* mean, however, that I can't have some sympathy for him, because I do.

I was obliged to inform the hospital what had happened. Of course they dismissed him immediately. In the few weeks that followed, I had reports that a small preponderance of petty thieving in a large number of departments on the South and West side of the campus had suddenly stopped. All the departments Dave cleaned in, as a matter of fact, and not just Dr Rafiq's. So, as I said, I see Dave on the estate now and then. He's still looking for work. But who would employ him now, with a police record for 'theft from employer'?

DNA

Just across a service road and, in the shadow of the great conker trees at this side of the campus, is 'H- Block'. Obviously named due to the shape of the building. A two-storey, pre-fabricated, post-war construction. One side faces South Road, and the other, the poplar trees, and brook. It's pretty dark down at this bottom end of the campus at night, and the area has therefore suffered a disproportionate amount of graffiti and vandalism. Kids from the estate across the main road occasionally congregate in the vicinity. There's a rope swing made from a garden hose hanging from a large tree over the brook close by. There's also a very wide steel pipe, which spans the brook, and is easy enough to use as a bridge, hence the kids getting across and causing problems. The buildings themselves are only used in the day time, on weekdays, and so added to the relatively poor lighting, during weekends there's no-one around to keep an eye out. There are too few decent CCTV cameras around these buildings, adding to their vulnerability.

'H-Block' is where prosthetic limbs are made and fitted. Wheelchairs abound in the building and clutter the corridors and doorways like shelled Daleks. Red ones, grey ones, black ones, yellow ones. Some marked with the hospital name, some brand new and expensive looking, others rather plain, scratched and sad. Some of these wheelchairs are quite obviously too old and exhausted to be worth much in monetary terms, but the newer models gleam in their more up-to-date sleekness and refined, ergonomic curves. Kids love them. Patients do too, of course, but kids probably more so. There's been a steady drip-drip of wheelchairs going missing from the campus over the years. They now have to be locked up, when once they would be left around, free for patients to use. At least one such wheelchair was stolen from 'H-Block' one night when the rear double fire doors were smashed in. Windows reinforced with wire mesh were smashed first, before the doors were forced. No-one will ever know how many kids managed to get in that night. More than two or three, that's for sure. The point of entry faced the brook, was out of view of any CCTV camera, and in deep shadow. The alarm had activated and security turned up, but their cursory glances as they drove by were not enough to see the damage to the door. The alarm had stopped, so they left, assuming it to be a false call. Probably a spider on the motion sensor.

The kids then had the place to themselves. They must have had a great time. The tracks in the floor certainly indicated this. All the corridors were lined with dozens of wheelchair tracks, up and down, round in circles, colliding with the walls, furniture and one another. They must have been in there for quite some time. I guessed they'd been having races with one another around the building and had decided to take one of the wheelchairs as a souvenir at the end of the night.

I spoke to the caretaker of the building, Colin, and he showed me how they'd gained entry. I noticed when they'd first smashed the windows in the fire doors one of them had cut themselves. There was blood on the glass in the remains of the windows. There was some smeared blood on the mat inside the door too where whoever it was had attempted to wipe their injury. Also a smear on one of the walls, a few yards inside the building. There had been no attempt to force any of the locked doors into the offices. Computers and other valuable items were inside these rooms. Whoever had broken in had obviously contented themselves with the wheelchairs and were not serious burglars. This seemed only to confirm my suspicions it was kids.

Scenes of crime officers attended and 'dusted for prints' as the movies describe it, with their silver nitrate powder. The marks, such as were left, were too smudged. Seventeen points of similarity are needed. I don't think they managed anywhere near that. But, swabs of blood were taken. From the glass, the mat, and the wall. It doesn't take a lot for DNA to be obtained. I had a result of sorts, which reached me only a few weeks later. DNA was recovered from the blood samples. Fantastic! But it didn't relate to anyone on the database!

Two years later, having just about forgotten the whole incident, I was sent several pages of forensic report from our Scenes of Crime department. A match had now been found. It took me a few moments to remember the job, it had been so long since I'd attended. A lad who lived across the main road had been detained for a minor shop-lifting offence a month before in the city centre and arrested. As with all our customers who pass through our doors now, his DNA was taken via a mouth swab on the end of a very long, purpose-made cotton-bud. This was sent off in a sealed plastic bag with a unique reference number and examined. Then it was entered into the national DNA database, along with his details. Having entered the system, a search was automatically carried out, and a 'hit' was reported.

Several years ago, when still a relatively new concept, we had hundreds of such DNA hits to deal with. The vast majority were burglary and auto-crime offences. If you are ever unfortunate enough to have your car stolen today, the police will ask you if you smoke. They have no vicarious interest in your health, or your bad habits, but they do need to know, for forensic reasons. The merest touch of the lips on a cigarette is enough to leave your DNA behind, on the filter. So if your car thief smokes when your vehicle is in his care and leaves his cigarette ends in the vehicle, then this is enough for us to feel his collar, so to speak! Even from spending a short time in a room, you can inadvertently leave your DNA behind. Hence crime scene visitors wearing those strange-looking white overalls with hoods and face masks, in order to avoid contamination. Certainly no-one who has possibly come into contact with witnesses or accused should ever enter a crime scene, as the remotest hint of contamination could cause doubt in the prosecution case, and the whole thing could be lost. Of course the main DNA hits the public get to know about are perhaps the more high profile murder cases, particularly ones which have been dormant for years. The so called 'cold cases'. The media often make headline news of such incidents, some of which are twenty or thirty years old or more. Imagine committing such a heinous crime and enjoying most of the rest of your life after the event, assuming you'd managed to escape justice, until one day the police come knocking at your door! The DNA doesn't even have to be yours. Your close relatives' DNA is very similar, and if they are detained, the search can also reveal close hits to them, close enough to arouse suspicion on the whole family. It has certainly transformed policing and is very impressive. It can also be used to clear as well as convict, of course. So it is a very useful piece of kit in the fight against crime. In my humble opinion, everyone in the country should be on the DNA database from birth.

So this young lad living near the hospital had left his DNA behind in 'H-Block', that night. I went to his address, but no-one was in. I left a note for him to bring himself, and an adult, to the police station. He was still only sixteen. Anyone under seventeen must have a parent, or other 'appropriate adult' present in interview. I remember Billy Reynolds brought his older brother, Michael, who was twenty-one. I took them both downstairs and formally placed Billy under arrest. Suspicion of burglary and theft. They requested the 'duty' solicitor: Whichever law firm was providing legal aid that day. Usually most regular criminals know the names and phone numbers of their solicitors in their heads, and it's usually the first thing they ask for. In fact, I've very often been greeted with the words, "You can fuck off 'till I've spoken to…" and the law firm, or even individual lawyer would be named. But Billy was quite new to this game, and so wasn't specific.

When the solicitor arrived we had our 'disclosure'. I told him about the DNA hit. Thirty minutes later I had an admission on tape. But an admission to the bare minimum, burglary with intent only, and not theft. I couldn't prove he'd stolen a wheelchair, or anything else, so, as I've said before, only the bare minimum is usually admitted. As he'd not yet been convicted of his shoplifting offence, and so had a clean record at that time, it was decided, taking into account the job was two years old, he should get a 'Caution'. So the custody sergeant gave him his telling off, and that was that. He refused to tell me who he'd been with that night, claiming he couldn't remember. There'd been no more such similar problems in those buildings since, and the crime was now detected. A reasonable outcome. Thanks to DNA!

COURAGE

I was sitting in the old security office, just prior to the move into the new one with all the wide screen monitors on the walls. Nathan had made me a coffee, and I was chatting to him while sipping it. There wasn't a lot happening, so I was about to plod down to South corridor to conduct a few follow-up enquiries. I like to visit the scene of each and every crime on the campus, whether I personally took the report or not, in order to see if security can be improved upon. It usually can, which is why I do it. I sit on the monthly hospital security committee, so these are the issues which I can raise in these meetings if necessary. It was a Saturday, so the campus was relatively quiet. The move to the new control room was imminent, so the office was a mess. The wood floor was black and brown, indicative of years of neglect and dirt. The chairs were threadbare and frankly dangerous to sit on. But all was to be replaced soon, so it didn't matter. The small CCTV monitors were still working and flicking around on their pre-programmed sweeps as usual. Nathan was twenty years of age. He was tall and slim, and he kept his hair short at the back and sides, with some length on the top, but flat, as though he was about to enlist. This is trendy, apparently. He spoke quickly, in a local accent, which caused me to sometimes have to say to him, 'Nathan, say all that again, but slower this time.' His partner had recently had a baby boy, their first, and he was still in the throes of paternal excitement which the new circumstances brought. He seemed to take more time off than he used to, that's for sure. Good for him.

We were discussing father-son relationships, and which local football team his son would be supporting. Crucial in a city where there are two very prominent soccer teams, each with a proud and lengthy history. I also discussed some of the cases I was dealing with at the hospital. Despite his youth, I found Nathan to be quite intuitive, and I enjoyed running ideas past him when I had a new case to investigate. He would make a decent police officer, if he only knew it. I may have told him this in the past, more than once, but his diffidence seemed to keep him where he was. Which was another reason for me to solicit his opinions. They were not only worthwhile, but it encouraged him to think along more positive lines.

Nathan was sitting with his back to the CCTV monitors and I was sitting facing him. The window to the office was on my left. It was quite a warm, sunny summer afternoon, so it was propped open at the top. There were other members of the security team on duty, but they were not in the building. Out on patrol no doubt. So there we were, Nathan and I, alone. As I sat there, espousing my worldly knowledge on the poor lad, there was a sudden and very loud *thwack!* sound from behind me and to my left. It seemed as though something had struck the window with tremendous force. I looked to see if it had been broken, but to my surprise, and relief, it hadn't. Nathan and I both briefly looked at one another and listened out for any further noise or voices. Nothing. Nathan muttered an inaudible stream of profanities, and stood up, looking towards the window. I remained in my chair and glanced at the window, trying to remain calm. Some sort of long metal pipe had fallen from the open window into the office, and onto a desk. One end of which was still sticking out of the window. It appeared to me to have probably fallen from the ceiling, but Nathan stated it had come through the open window. In other words then, it had been *pushed* through the window from outside. As it was on the next desk, it had probably missed hitting me by only a few feet.

I didn't see the length of pipe fall from the window. I didn't see anyone outside. It had gone quiet again, so I felt no need to get up and investigate. I still entertained the possibility it had fallen quite innocently. There was a lot of building work going on at the time. It was probably some loose material incorrectly positioned by the builders. I remained in my seat. We resumed our conversation. Less than a minute later we both heard loud banging from outside. It wasn't immediately outside, but somewhere near the main entrance doors, twenty yards away. 'It's kids. Or someone trying to get in,' Nathan said. A concerned expression swept over his face and the look he gave me was a clear indication that he wanted me to do something. Or at the very least *say*, something. More banging. Then more. There was most definitely someone there. I'd have to get up and investigate. If someone was bashing the doors intent on damaging them, if not already damaged, I may be forced to make an arrest to prevent a breach of the peace, or for offences of threatening behaviour. I then realised the length of pipe in the window was likely to be the same person, or persons, now banging on the doors.

I stood up, took a deep breath, and walked to the door of the office. I straightened up my stab vest, and my utility belt, then felt the reassuring steel touch of my baton and my speed cuffs. I stepped into the corridor and began walking towards the main doors. Little or no time to summon up any adrenalin. I'd made the very quick transition from being relaxed to fight mode in a few short seconds. This can be very challenging at times. Apparently quite stressful too. If the rush of adrenalin isn't then used up somehow, it can supposedly be injurious to health. Response policing can be like this often. Driving about at high speed around the city, being the first on the scene at anything from a pub fight to a house fire, or a man and woman at each other's throats. It can eventually shred the nerves a little. My wife remembers several occasions when I was on response duties, years ago, when I'd wake up with a start, in the middle of the night, fists clenched, babbling orders at shadows in the bedroom. It can certainly be the most difficult and under-rated aspect of policing. Usually the preserve of new recruits, the younger, more resilient police officers. Not many old cops stay on response.

So it was that I was having to summon up some raw courage as the adrenalin had not had time to kick in. I wasn't aware I possessed any, that is until an incident I was called to when I was quite young in service. Don't misunderstand me here, I'm not a hero. Far from it. In fact, I thought I was firmly in the opposite camp and a screaming coward. I believed this even long after the incident which tested me more than most others I've been to, but now realise I wasn't actually in the throes of cowardice at all. Being ordered into a life threatening situation, cold, unprepared, is the worst kind of experience. I will just spend a few minutes describing this particular incident before we return to the matter in the security office.

I was aware, one hot summer afternoon, as I was minding my own business in my own police station, that some miles away an incident was running. It was a serious incident too, as I could hear snippets of it on the radio. Some drunken, violent man had barricaded himself into a flat and was threatening everyone who came near. Not really my concern, as I'd heard plenty of police officers were at the scene and it was nowhere near my patrol area. More and more police officers were being sent over there, all afternoon, as the time passed. It was not a huge surprise then to be asked to travel over there in a large van with two other colleagues. Transport duties, or crowd control, I thought. We pulled up in our van near the address and put on our padding and riot helmets. Up until then there was still nothing unusual in this. Looking around, most cops present were similarly dressed. There must have been twenty or more police officers crouching down outside the man's flat, behind walls, and hiding behind vehicles. Apparently he was armed, though not with a firearm, or so it was thought, but with a 'variety of weapons', as they were described. There was some urgency too, as it became clear there were children in the flat, hiding upstairs, obviously at risk.

The Inspector in charge came over to us, just at the point where we'd finished putting on the riot gear and were about to pick up some shields. He was a corpulent man, very overweight, with a bright red face. I noticed he was sweating profusely, but thought this was due to his size, and the heat. We didn't know him, Steve, John and I, but we knew who he was. He walked straight up to us and gave us an order I'll never forget. I remember his exact words, as though spoken to me yesterday:

"Glad you're here lads." He said, looking very intently at us. "I want *you* three to go in and get him."

What? I thought. What?! I'm sure John and Steve thought the same too, looking around. Why us? More importantly, why *me*? *This wasn't even my area!* I shouldn't even be here! Get some other bugger to do it! This can't be right! But not one of the three of us actually said anything out loud. It seemed all the other cops knew what we'd just been told. They looked as if they did, as they were all looking at us. Or was this my imagination? Did I *think* they were looking at us, waiting for one or all three of us to refuse, or even turn and walk away, back to our van? What were the consequences of such a refusal? Disciplinary action? Shame? Embarrassment? A reputation? Yes, if we refused, if I refused, then the name would stick. It would be with me for years, if not for the rest of my service. There was no option.

We picked up our shields from the back of the van and Steve locked it. He put the keys in his pocket and we walked towards the flat. As we drew nearer I could hear loud, drunken, abusive shouts from inside. It was on the ground floor of a four-storey block. All the front windows were smashed. There were items of broken furniture strewn around on the grass in front of the building. The cops closest to the flat looked in real fear. The front door to the flat was apparently locked. A colleague was to force it for us, before the three of us were to rush in and grab him. Sounds great. I just hoped the idea worked. Steve, John and I stood at the door. If it was bashed in quickly we'd maintain an element of surprise. We knew he was in the living room, so it was straight in and first right. Another colleague nudged up against me with a new 'enforcer' in his hands. The heavy steel instrument used to batter doors down. They were relatively new at the time and I'd not seen one used for real before. 'Ready?' he said. 'Yes' we replied, almost in perfect unison. The cop took a swing with the enforcer and it struck the wooden door with a dead thud. It didn't move. He raised it quickly and struck it again. Still nothing. The shouting inside the flat had stopped. Then another strike on the door. The wood began to crack and splinter. I heard the man inside resume his shouting. He now knew we were coming in to get him.

Finally the door collapsed enough for us to clamber in. There were items of furniture in the hallway, and it was not easy to climb over the debris with the long shields in hand. I lowered my visor and was immediately aware of the quickening of my breathing. The Perspex fogged immediately, so I had to reach up and raise it a little, otherwise I wouldn't have been able to see at all. We'd trained for incidents such as this in the 'mad man in the room' scenario. As a concession to political correctness, the procedure is now called 'angry man in the room'. Two or three police officers in the appropriate garb using the long shields would rush at the perpetrator – in training it would be a well-built colleague wielding a baseball bat and shouting obscenities – and push him bodily up against a wall, thereby disabling him. That's the theory. It seemed to work quite well in training! Most of the time anyway. Nudging ourselves down the hallway, lifting the heavy shields over the numerous obstacles in our path, we drew nearer to the door into the living area. We could hear the man shouting. He seemed to be singing too. Or at least that's what it sounded like. I could hear martial music playing above some gruff, heavily accented obscenities. Then I realised what the music was. It was German wartime propaganda, interspersed with some particularly loud, ranting Hitler speeches. His shouting was intermixed with those of a very loud Adolf Hitler, to the extent I couldn't tell which was which. They seemed to be competing with one another. The man was obviously trying to imitate the Führer in his own rough, colloquial English version of the German language, and so it sounded more like a Welsh miner after ten pints of beer. No offence to Welsh miners!

We still hadn't seen this man yet, despite hearing him, so we trudged up closer to the open living room door. The cheap wooden door was only hanging from one bottom hinge, and was holed in several places. It also looked like it had been slashed at and battered with an axe, or something similar. I remember it was at this point that John, who was in the middle of the three of us, said to Steve and me: 'When we get in the room, we'll rush him, right? Straight away, yeah?' We both agreed, and readied ourselves for stepping into the room. At that point I do remember thinking to myself, 'How did I get here? How the hell did I get myself into this predicament?!' We shuffled into the doorway, together, then quickly into the room. For an instant we had our first look at the angry man. A white male, about forty, of only average build, short black hair, and a few days stubble. He was wearing a green army-type shirt. There was a swastika armband on his left arm. In his left hand was a half-drunk bottle of bourbon. It was the item in his right hand which concentrated our minds the most though. There was a very large blade, like a long kitchen knife or a machete, taped firmly to the end of a six foot long wooden broom handle.

So this is it, I thought. This *could* be it. In this instant as we entered the room, before charging at the man, a thousand thoughts flashed around inside my head. What an ignominious way to go, and in such an awful place as this! I thought of all the other, more exotic places in the world I'd seen, and all the close scrapes I'd been in. I'd lived in a war-zone in the Middle East for eighteen months and been caught in air-raids. I'd hitch-hiked across Europe and Australia and had some pretty lucky escapes, but here I was, in this shitty little flat, facing this deranged Neo-Nazi. If I tripped and fell at his feet, I might be hacked to death, or sliced up like a piece of ham. I remember thinking, telling myself not to fall over. To look where I was going. To keep up with John and Steve. Our only chance was to arrive at our target *together*, in unison, and over-power him with the brute force of three against one. It was so important the three of us worked together. As we rushed at him, I heard the man start to shout at us. 'I'll kill the fucking lot of you,' or similar. He didn't quite manage to finish what he was saying. Before he could level his makeshift spear in our direction, we'd made contact with him. As the *Horst Wessel* filled our ears, the bottle in his left hand struck one of the heavy shields. Bourbon splashed wildly out the neck of the bottle over the Perspex, the glass clunking loudly against it as it did so. Then the weapon in his right hand was flattened harmlessly against the shields, as indeed he was. We pushed at him as hard as we could. Within a second or two he was pressed firmly and immovably against the back wall of the living room, crushed tightly against our relentless pushing. He was trying to scream at us, but his face was contorted and compressed to such an extent he couldn't shout or even breathe. Then suddenly the man was gone, buried beneath a writhing, frenzied mass of police uniforms, pulling and shouting at him. He was cuffed and trussed up with leg restraints and dragged like a prize turkey out of the room. All within a few short seconds.

So, that was an example of what I would humbly describe as 'courage'. You may disagree, of course. But for years afterward I thought I'd been cowardly that day. I didn't discuss the incident. I thought that because of my fearful thoughts, I'd been cowardly. But had I? I went in and did the job, didn't I? It took a colleague to point out to me much later that fear is natural, and a good thing in such circumstances. It can make you more careful, clear-headed and determined. We'd been sent into the situation cold, with little or no time to raise any adrenalin, or even act on instinct. We followed orders. We simply had to do it. And we did. It's not cowardly to feel fear, as I thought it was. It's acknowledging it, and then despite this overcoming it, and getting the job done, which can amount to it being described as a courageous action. And I was right about John and Steve. Much the same had flashed through their minds too. But we didn't talk about it.

As in the afternoon I'd began to describe, when Nathan and I were in the security office, just the two of us. Someone had thrown a steel pipe through the open window, probably at me, and I was walking towards the doors to investigate. Nathan was behind me, I turned the left hand corner and walked towards the main entrance. The doors appeared undamaged. I was surprised and relieved. From the noises I'd heard earlier, I'd expected at least *some* damage. But there was none. I couldn't see anyone outside, so I pressed the exit button on the wall which opened the doors. I had to go out and have a look around. I touched the top of my steel baton in its leather holder, but as yet didn't draw it out. Despite a probable cool exterior, I was readying myself for a physical confrontation. I didn't consciously remember my brush with the angry Neo-Nazi all those years ago, but I thought I may be in for something similar.

As I stepped out of the doorway I was mercilessly set upon by two men from my left hand side. They both shouted:

"WOAH!" in a loud shriek, together, as they leapt out at me.

Their arms were raised above their heads and they were wildly flailing them around in my direction. I immediately responded by instinctively adopting a fighting stance. Left foot forward, and most of my weight on my back foot. I lowered my centre of gravity and raised my arms. I formed my hands into a kind of Kung-Fu chop type of arrangement in front of me and also let out a deep, bellowing, extremely loud "WOAH!" of my own to counter theirs. I'm not sure where this type of display is hidden in the Home Office self-defence manual! There we were, three men, shouting and flailing our arms about in an instant of surprise and terror. Suddenly, and before we made any contact with one another, my two attackers were laughing hysterically. They were laughing so much I thought they were about to collapse onto the ground. It was Shaun and Andy, two security guards! I let out a rather rude and unprofessional expletive and just stood there, deflated and hugely embarrassed. But also relieved, of course. I was angry with myself for being taken in, but happy, eventually, to see the funny side. Fortunate for them I'd not deployed my CS before checking who it was. I would never do that though. This was a perfect *Youtube* clip that was never recorded. Shaun and Andy made some profuse apologies, as they were hoping Nathan would have been their victim. They claimed to have been unaware I was sitting in the office at all. Never mind, no harm done. Apologies accepted. But they might just have to watch out though, one dark night, when they are out on their own...

WARNING SIGNALS

It is indicative of the relationship I have with many of the hospital security team that they feel able to abuse me the way they do. But as I have already stated, our relationship is quite a satisfying one of mutually pragmatic, professional exploitation. Shaun himself has helped me on numerous occasions. At least once he was there for me in a particular situation which could easily have turned very nasty. We'd all been on the lookout for two 'hoodies' who had been plaguing the campus for several weeks. Numerous cars had been broken into, always in the same very crude and amateurish manner, but so far we had not managed to apprehend the pair of reprobates. We had some CCTV images of them, from the back, wandering around one of the staff car parks. They seemed to be very cool in the way they conducted themselves, or very careless, and appeared to be on a Sunday afternoon stroll rather than a crime spree. They would cause huge amounts of reckless damage to the vehicles they attacked. Using some sort of sharp implement they would ram this tool into the door locks very forcefully in the hope the door would eventually open. If this failed, as it usually did, they would try to prize open the door by jamming the instrument down the rubber seal inside the window frame. Quite often the window would shatter under the strain, allowing them brief access to the vehicle before their inward reaching thieving arms would set off the alarm. Meanwhile the door frame was badly damaged and a new door was needed. But they usually had enough time to steal the sat-nav and anything else left in the vehicle. I'd seen the CCTV we had of the pair breaking into a car a few days before. As they calmly made their way across this particular car park, it was clear at one point they were holding hands. They were both of similar height and build, and appeared to be wearing similar clothing, that of jeans, trainers and hoodies. So these two were probably boyfriend and girlfriend under the unisex clothes. Or two males, or females, in a gay relationship.

It was a Friday afternoon, less than an hour before I was due to finish for the weekend. I'd been busy all week and was looking forward to Friday night in my local pub. My police mobile phone rang. It was Shaun:

"Jonathan, they're back. Those two we're after. They've just gone into the same staff car park."

"Right," I replied. "I'll get a van. I'll be with you in a few minutes. Keep an eye on them!"

I knew full well that if I made an arrest, or two arrests, at this time of day, I'd still be at work late into the evening. I could have told Shaun to ring '999'. But then I wanted these two myself. They were upsetting me, and my crime figures! How dare they keep wandering onto *my* patch as they were doing, breaking into cars willy-nilly! Who did they think they were?! So I took some vehicle keys from the key safe, ran down the back stairs of the station and started up my little police van. Foolishly I didn't tell any of my colleagues what I was doing. Within a few short minutes I was pulling into North Road. I saw Shaun with Julie, one of the security supervisors, driving towards me in their security van. We stopped our vehicles side by side in the road and wound down our windows. 'They've gone out of the site, down the road,' Shaun said, indicating behind me. I turned my vehicle around and drove back out of the campus. A hundred yards down the road the two were turning into a side-street.

I pulled up just past them and got out of the van. I opened the side sliding door and introduced myself.

"Would you mind if I had a quick word with you please?"

I said, as I ushered them both into the back seat of my outwardly small, but surprisingly capacious police van. I remember thinking I probably sounded rather vague, a little like Sgt Wilson, John Le Measurier's character in 'Dad's Army'.

They were a male and a female, as I saw their faces for the first time. The female said nothing, but the male replied:

"Why, what's up, officer?"

"I'll tell you in a minute."

I replied, continuing to be vague, hoping they'd remain civil and co-operative. We were now fifty yards up a side-street and largely away from public view.

Just at that moment, and before the two had decided on whatever course of action they may have been considering, Shaun drew up behind me in his security van, engine revving, with Julie in the front seat, like 'Starsky and Hutch', or more probably, looking at Julies' shoulder length blonde hair, 'Cagney and Lacey'. Shaun immediately jumped out and approached quickly, covering the ground between his van and the three of us with long, determined strides.

"You okay, Jonathan?" he said, his yellow reflective coat and uniform probably giving the impression he was at the very least *connected* to the police force, if not actually part of it. Shaun is not a small chap either, and his demeanour at that moment was one of eager, reassuring self-confidence.

"Yes, fine. I'm just going to have a chat to these two."

And again I ushered them into the van. Whether they had been thinking of running, or fighting, I'll never know. At that moment, having probably made a quick assessment of their situation, they decided together to sit in my van voluntarily. Once inside the van, I spoke to them at the open sliding door.

"Where have you been this afternoon?"

"Just to the shops , mate." The male said.

"Not the hospital then?" I said, fishing for an incriminating response.

"Hospital? No. Well. We might have walked through it a bit. Why?"

"What's your name, mate?" I asked the male. I'd not met him before. Looking at their clothing, it was clear they matched the description of the pair we we'd been after for weeks.

"Jimmy Smith," he replied.

"What's your name, love?" I said to the female.

"Tina Harris," she said, after some hesitation. She seemed nervous. He seemed calm and confident.

"Have you got anything on you?" I said to them both.

She was carrying a plastic carrier bag, holding it in both hands, and I took it from her lap as she was sitting on the back seat with her associate. I opened the bag, out of their view, and showed the contents to Shaun. There was a very long, very sturdy, new-looking screw-driver, with a large, blue and grey rubber handle. I shut the sliding door, with the two of them inside.

"It's definitely them," I said to Shaun.

"Oh God yes," he replied. "Do you want me to follow you to the station?" he added.

"Yes, can do. I'll take them both in, now. Thanks."

I sat in the driver's seat and turned the van around. As we drove up the hill towards the station, the male asked:

"Where are we going, mate?"

I replied:

"I'm just going to take you both home, right?"

"Yeah, yeah, great. Ta," came the unsuspecting reply.

I realised I could have problems with the two of them so I'd decided to use a little subterfuge. They were okay now, but if I told them they were under arrest, in Training School fashion, then the situation could very rapidly deteriorate. I had a sudden realisation that I should never have placed myself at such risk. I didn't know who these two were. I was driving a van with these two people sat behind me, with nothing between the back of my head and them. I kept up a conversation of mainly vague, palliative remarks until we arrived at the station. At the electric gates to the station I managed to swipe my warrant card and drive in before another question came from behind me. Once inside the secure grounds of the station yard, I then told them the bad news:

"You're both nicked on suspicion of theft from vehicles, at the hospital, and going equipped."

I cautioned them. To my amazement, neither of them protested their innocence, or shouted, swore, or cursed at me, as was usual in these circumstances. In fact they were very quiet. I must have caught them on a good day. I was lucky. How lucky I didn't fully appreciate until a few minutes later.

I searched the male once he was stood in front of the custody sergeant at the charge desk in the cells. To my horror, he was also in possession of a 'Stanley' knife. A very sharp knife. Also a glass cutter in the form of a small hammer. And some cannabis. I'd had this chap in the van behind me, and all the time he had a knife and a hammer in his pockets! I was surprised and relieved there'd not been any trouble on the way back to the station. Not as relieved as I was once I'd checked him on the computer. He admitted, while he was being 'booked in' by the custody sergeant, that he'd been using false details. His real name was Robert Vernon Delano Tucker. In Britain, the Police National Computer contains the records of all persons detained by the police. Descriptions, addresses, associates, all their court appearances and so on. It also flags up, on the front page of any such record, in bold red writing, any 'Warning Signals'. If one of our customers has been known to be violent in the past, tried to escape, or are suspected of carrying a contagious disease, etc., then this information is listed as one of these 'Warning Signals'. For obvious reasons. I've never seen anyone have more than one or two of these on their record. Until I met Mr Tucker. He had clearly been collecting them. He had the following 'Warning Signals': VIOLENT. ESCAPER. DRUGS. SUICIDAL. WEAPONS. AILMENT. I'd never seen so many on one person's record! I hadn't even handcuffed this man in the back of my police vehicle!

Mr Tucker was wiry and short. A career criminal, thirty years of age and long-term heroin addict. He wore thick, bottle-bottom glasses. But he'd obviously upset some police officers on some previous occasions! I must have caught him on a good day. What an idiot I'd been! It became clear why he'd tried to use another name, too. He was wanted by two other, neighbouring police forces for similar auto-crime offences. Dozens of other offences, in fact. If anyone had ever had a good reason to assault a police officer and escape custody, it was him! Tina and Robert were indeed boyfriend and girlfriend. Tina was released without charge. He did the gentlemanly thing and took the rap for everything I had on him at the hospital. He claimed he had instigated it all, and she was an unwilling participant. So be it. She denied it all anyway. I charged him with a clutch of offences and he was remanded in custody. I finally went home just after midnight. I missed the pub, but was very pleased with the evening's events. Colleagues in the other police areas collected him the next day. Eventually he went to prison for nine months, as far as I can remember. I just reflected on how stupid I'd been, and how fortunate. I'd had a very lucky escape that day.

RACE

Race is a highly contentious subject. I doubt there is anything more so. If I were to accrue a thousand wonderful years of uninterrupted public service, achieve greatness through it, and win huge praise from the highest in the land, it would suddenly and inevitably all count for nought if I were even once to be heard using the 'N' word. I'd be sacked on the spot and marched off the premises. I'm reluctant to even *write* the 'N' word in full, it has become so absolutely verboten. In fact it is listed at the Home Office now as a proscribed word. I used to hear it a lot, in the early days of my service. Along with its many equally insulting derivatives, such as 'nig-nog', 'coon', 'wog' and so on. Mainly from older officers and particularly those grey-haired, beer-bellied colleagues in the CID, now long since retired and/or deceased. Such as things were in those days. That's just how it was. There was nothing personal about it. There was just as much sexism as there was racism. Female officers made the tea and looked after kids. That was it. In hindsight, there was probably widespread and completely unchallenged usage of every single modern '- ism' going. It's probably conceited of me to say now that I actually never used such words myself. But it's true. Certainly not at work. I would never admit to any occasion when such a word as 'nigger' passed my lips. Not even many years ago, when drunk, in a pub somewhere, while telling a bad joke. There's no reason or excuse. There is no doubt as to how offensive the word is. I've not heard it in police circles, both on and off duty, for quite some years. Rightly so, I hear you say. But is one slip-up enough to destroy a career? One single slip of the tongue? Well, whether you think so or not, in the current politically correct environment, in the public sector it will almost certainly get you the sack. Not only this, but could even get you a term of imprisonment. What, just for using that word? Well, actually, yes. It's not just a word, of course. It's an emblem, a badge, a symbol, a mindset. You may as well wear a swastika on your arm. By using that word, and words similar to it, you are vocalising your inner thoughts. You must be a racist. End of. But are there any exceptions?

I was called to one of the units at the hospital on just such a matter. Initially I was asked to give some advice to the department head, over the phone. I didn't feel entirely comfortable discussing race issues in this way, so decided to visit in person. On arrival, I immediately detected reluctance on the part of the manager I spoke to, Barbara, about the whole matter. I'd seen Barbara before, when investigating another, entirely different problem, some months before, in the same department. I sat down on a rather plush leather chair in her office, a few feet from her desk, and listened intently to her problem. I cradled my police helmet in my hands, and began to remove my leather gloves as she spoke. Barbara was my type, I suppose. Or at least would have been, twenty years before. Quite tall, slim, with blonde hair which fell about her shoulders in large golden curls. Freckles and blue eyes. Quite pretty. She spoke with a gentle, and softly melodic, soothing voice. The type which I imagined could easily send me to sleep on a quiet afternoon, perhaps while watching her doing some ironing, with Radio 4 and

'Woman's Hour' humming in the background. Or am I being sexist here? She fumbled about for a while before she came to the point.

"One of the staff has called another one a golly-wog. Well, not *called* it them as such. But they said they *looked* like one."

I'd not heard the expression for years. I'm afraid to admit that at first, just for a fleeting second, I found the situation mildly amusing. Only for a second though. How did this happen? I quickly reminded myself of the potential consequences and seriousness of it. Not to mention the probable hurt that may have been inflicted on the recipient of the remark. Under Home Office guidelines, this perfectly fitted the definition of a 'Racial Incident'. It was a public place and someone had been racially abused. In fact, the only place in the UK currently exempt from the law in this respect was inside a dwelling. I asked what happened, and in what context the expression was used, and Barbara replied:

"One of our older members of staff just called her, well, said it to her."

"Who said what? What happened, exactly?" I said, reaching for my pocket book.

"Stanley is one of our oldest members of staff. He's been here for years. More than thirty-odd years at least. He said to Lisbet, who's not been here very long, 'We used to call you lot golly-wogs. That's what we used to call you golly-wogs.' That's what he said to her apparently. She's made a formal complaint."

"Did he say anything else?" I asked.

"Yes, I'm afraid so. He said 'You look just like one of those golly-wogs. You ought to get your hair cut. It makes you look just like a golly-wog.'

I took a deep breath, sighed a little, and opened my pocket book. I wrote the time and date, and what Barbara had just told me. She carried on:

"Lisbet's from Africa. I'm not sure exactly where. She only started here last year. She's very highly qualified. She speaks very good English, and understood what was being said to her, obviously. She took offence. Apparently she reported it to her line manager, who's also black, but he didn't do anything about it, so she says. I think this made her even more angry."

"Right," I said, "I'll deal with it. I'll need to see them both at some point. Where are they now, do they both work in the same department?"

I was initially hoping to 'bang their heads together' to use the old expression, and speak to them directly about it, each in turn, and together. I hoped an apology would possibly suffice. Maybe there had been a misunderstanding? Perhaps Lisbet had heard wrongly? Were the remarks said deliberately to cause insult? I needed to know exactly what had happened.

"Yes, they do. Stanley's here, but Lisbet's not here at the moment. I understand she's gone to her local police station to report it."

"What?" I said, incredulous. If another cop spoke to her it would completely restrict my options, particularly if he or she committed it straight to paper and gave it a crime number.

"When did she go to the police?" I asked, for some reason trying to read the time from a non-existent clock on the wall.

"She went home this morning. She was upset. She stated she was going there straight away."

I picked up my lid and thanked Barbara for her time. I'd taken full details of their names, and those of potential witnesses. I made my way back to the station. Sure enough, around four hours earlier, a crime number had been generated with Lisbet Rosemary Samuels as the aggrieved, and Stanley Albert Waterford as the 'offender'. Lisbet was twenty-two. Stanley was sixty-four.

The next morning I returned to the unit to see Barbara. I wanted to get this sorted out as quickly as possible. I'd obtained a copy of the crime report. The police officer Lisbet had seen the day before had taken a detailed five-page statement. Other racial references were mentioned, by other members of staff, mostly of a trivial and irrelevant nature. But she was mostly insulted by, and wanted to complain the most, about what Stanley had said. I explained to Barbara the rather limited options, now the matter had been formally recorded as a crime. I did think of all the other crimes I'd dealt with at the hospital, and the triviality of this one brief remark made by one member of staff to another. But it was a crime. It needed to be investigated. An 'offender' had also been named.

Lisbet was at home. She was apparently too traumatised to come to work. Stanley was there though. He'd never missed a days' work in his life, apparently. I asked to see him. I took out some police contemporaneous notepaper, just as Stanley entered the room, in company with his union rep. I introduced myself, we shook hands and I invited him to sit down at the table I was seated at with Barbara.

"I've got to ask you some questions, Stanley. Do you understand?"

"Oh yes, yes, of course, fire away, young man, yes." He looked up at me, his eyes wide open and pouring out great sloshing buckets of naïve sincerity.

I cautioned him, with the full police warning to suspects, which we are obliged to issue everyone prior to questioning them about an offence. I also explained his rights too, which are equally, if not more lengthy. Then I carried on:

"Stanley. Do you know a work colleague called Lisbet?"

"Lisbet? Yes, yes I do. Lovely girl. She's lovely. Me and her get on very well you know. She's from Africa."

"Yes I know, Stanley. How long have you known her?"

"Well, I think she started here last year. She did, didn't she Barbara?" As he looked across at Barbara. Barbara returned a smile and nodded, edging an uncomfortable glance in my direction.

"Stanley, a few times you've said something to her which she's been offended by. Do you remember what you said?"

"Offended? She never said anything. What was it, what did I say that offended her? I'm sorry if I've said anything that's upset her. Oh dear. What was it, what did I say?"

He seemed genuinely puzzled. He looked around the room at the faces gathered around the table, as if to gain some clue as to what he'd done. He seemed completely unaware as to why he was being questioned. I decided to get to the point:

"Stanley, do you know the word 'golly-wog'? Have you ever used this expression?"

"Oh, I see. Yes. We used to call people like her, Lisbet I mean, gollies. Do you remember? Years ago. We used to, didn't we? We don't use it now, it's old-fashioned. You can't call people that now, can you, no. I was just telling her about it. I did say it to her, yes. She does look a bit like one, doesn't she? I told her she ought to get her hair cut. It made her look like a golly. Why? Am I in trouble for it?"

Barbara and I looked at one another. No. Stanley, no, I thought. You can't call people that nowadays. And yes, you are in trouble.

I had a confession on paper. An 'offender' had admitted a crime to me, and I had it written down. So why wasn't I jumping for joy? I concluded the interview. All present, including Stanley, signed the notes. Stanley was ushered out of the room. I spoke to Barbara briefly, before I left the department. I had to see other potential witnesses before I could pass the file to the next link in the prosecution chain. Barbara and I worked together on the matter for the following few days. Reluctant witnesses were seen. Twelve in all. Most stated they hadn't heard the alleged incident at all. A minority did. It seemed Stanley had indeed called Lisbet a 'golly-wog'. Their conversation had been overheard and it included jam jars, a famous brand of marmalade and modern acceptability. So there was some context to it. But he *did* say it to her. I obtained statements from all of them, positive and negative. A very time-consuming undertaking. Days of work turned into weeks of work. I thought of all the far more serious crimes I'd been involved in at the hospital. And this. Eventually, after gathering all the necessary paperwork, the file was an inch thick. I submitted it all in the usual way for a decision. It went from the police station to the local prosecuting authority.

After two weeks I'd heard nothing. This was very unusual. I made some phone calls and email enquiries with the prosecutors. I was told the local prosecuting team was unable, or unwilling to make a decision on the matter. It had been referred to senior prosecutors in London. A further three weeks passed and I finally had my decision. I expected it to be returned 'No action' or similar. At the very worst, Stanley was to be issued a police caution, or so I thought. I was utterly shocked when the result came through: Charge Stanley with two counts of racially aggravated public order offences.

Stanley was suspended from work. I prepared the charges. He came into the station with his son. His son was furious. 'Haven't you lot got better things to do than pursue an old man for making a silly remark?!' or words to that effect. He had a point. I charged him and he was processed like a criminal, despite the fact he'd never been in trouble before, in all his long life. Once charged with a criminal offence, the hospital sacked him. It's policy.

He appeared in court a few weeks later. He was pleading guilty. I wasn't in court, but I suspect the magistrates were unsure as to what, if any 'punishment' they should issue him. To this end, I was sent a message from the court. It had been adjourned pending a request from the court that I ask the aggrieved if she would agree to Stanley being issued with a 'Caution'. I'd never heard of this happening in this way before. A day after receiving this request from the court I rang Lisbet. But she was adamant. She stated she'd been in touch with some Race Equality groups and other similar organizations she'd discovered on the internet. She therefore refused to accept any leniency for Stanley.

As we are now 'victim led', I passed this decision back to the court. It should have had some influence. Stanley reappeared in court a few weeks later. For whatever reason, this time he stood before a judge, rather than a magistrate. I was told the result by email a few days later. My first thoughts were of all the hours and hours of painstaking work I'd undertaken to get Stanley to court. I also thought of the many professionals involved on the side of the prosecution who must have laboured for hours over their law books to arrive at the decision they did. Their decision was hidden in long pages of legal flannel they'd sent back to me, early in the enquiry, which was utterly pejorative and entirely denuded of emotion, or the faintest whiff of sympathy for Stanley. So it all came to a point, months later, with a judge making the final decision as to what to do with him. The little old chap who was physically half the size of the woman he'd offended so badly, who was as broad in circumference as she was tall. The judge must have seen something which no-one else all along the prosecution chain had seen. He threw the whole thing out. No case to answer. Stanley was given an 'Unconditional Discharge'.

Stanley had never been in court before. The realisation of what was happening eventually had a profound effect on him. He was unable to return to work. He'd been destroyed. I'm reasonably sure the remarks he made were not in any way meant to cause any alarm or distress. But the law states there doesn't necessarily need to be any *intent* for the offence to be complete. By the time the process was over, after more than six months, Stanley had reached retirement age. But he'd left, or rather been dismissed, under a dark cloud, after thirty-six years loyal hard work in public service. No party to celebrate his retirement. No 'leaving do'. Nothing. As for Lisbet. The last I heard she was still off work, too traumatised to return. On full pay. Considering legal action against her employers.

MATERNITY

From the top of 'chapel hill' the service road swings around to the left between the various out-patients blocks and joins North Road. The Outpatients buildings are more seventies concrete sectional buildings, one and two storeys high. One of the lower floors has been painted a bright pink on the outside but, other than this, the buildings are particularly non-descript but functional. There's a bright new building on the left, formally opened with great ceremony several years ago by HRH The Prince of Wales. I remember the build up to his visit when the staff found out he was due to call in at the campus. There were some members of staff who insisted they were not in the least interested in him or 'the likes of him' and said they were just not bothered about being around and seeing him. Until the day of the visit, that is. Granted, a lot of staff carried on with their duties, they had to, but those who saw him in the flesh stopped and stared, just like the rest of us. If nothing else, he's a media star, as they all are.

Walking up towards the new maternity department there are still some old red-brick buildings surviving. Ones which are still in use. Others have gone, and like in other places, are now car parks. Maternity needs plenty of car parking space. The new maternity building is huge. It includes a 'patient hotel', and the building is not unlike a hotel, both inside and out. It could easily be one of those in a popular chain of hotels, and you could imagine the place standing proudly alone in acres of park land, set back up a sweeping tree-lined driveway.

I've been quite busy in maternity. Even criminals have babies. Criminals' partners have babies. Hospitals and, in particular, the maternity department, is one of the last places in the UK where people from all classes and social strata are forced to mix together. Maternity provision is, on the whole, excellent, with the free-at-point-of-use health service. So there's little real need to pay for exclusivity. At the time of writing this, the chances are, if you didn't get your own private room, at no cost to yourself, you would be in a small ward of no more than three or four ladies. But as I said, criminals have babies. You yourself may be perfectly middle-class. But the person in the next bed may not be. Not a problem, in itself, unless you are a hopeless snob. Or have pots of money. Or both! But a real problem if the female in the next bed is a career criminal, and probably addicted to heroin. This can be a real eye-opener to some. It's not just the woman too. She's likely to have some very strange visitors. All of the same ilk. A further unwanted crash course into the solipsism of the great British underclass. Of course the staff are aware of these potential problems. But they are unwilling or unable to pass judgement on their clientele. Unless you know them as individuals, and speak to them in confidence behind closed doors, as I do. It's not that they are naïve. They do know who these people are. The staff knew full well what a certain patient was like when she stayed with them, albeit only briefly, for two days recently. The first I knew about what had happened was when I saw two calls on our computer from ladies who had gone home with their new babies to find cash and credit cards missing from their purses. They'd both contacted the police separately and independently of one another once they realised they'd been victims. But the message read they'd both stayed in the same ward. Even as I walked along North corridor, on my way to the ward to investigate, I was informed of further, similar incidents. Complaints of theft in that particular ward started to reach me almost hourly on that first day. I made it known to security and my own control room that I would be interested in any such reports. I was quickly inundated with reports of theft and suspicious activity.

Outside visiting hours the wards are closed, so I swiped my way past the doors and into the department. As a habit and professional courtesy, I always seek out the ward manager in the first instance. Even before speaking to victims. In this case, Jennifer *was* matronly and a little austere. She was a short, round figure, with thick ankles and huge bust like a great over-hanging cliff strapped tightly into her uniform. She spoke very quickly and kept asking my opinion, 'What do you think, well, what do *you* think?' and so on, seemingly in between everything I said. Understandably she was very concerned. Reports of thefts in the previous two days were reaching double figures. It was as though a hurricane had blown through her department and cut through everyone's possessions, taking half of them with it. I declined a cup of coffee, as I sensed the urgency of the situation. The first thing I asked her was for her assessment and whether she had any suspicions. Luckily, I had met Jennifer on some previous occasions, so she obviously felt able to be more candid with me than if I'd been an entirely new face.

There was a small ward of four ladies. Well, three ladies, and a female. A particular female. The three ladies in the ward had all been victims. Some other ladies in the wards immediately neighbouring this ward had also been victims. One lady found her own handbag in the rest room at the end of the corridor, in the shower tray, open, with the contents scattered around on the floor. The only person not a victim was the female in bed two called Lara Norman. She was very tall, and very thin, with long, bright red straggly hair. Apart from her bump, of course. She looked like she had a basketball stuffed under her clothing. She had very bad skin, which was greasy and very spotty. Some of this may have been her age, as she was only eighteen at the time, but I've no doubt her apparent ill health was mainly due to her lifestyle. Despite her pregnancy she was constantly shuffling out the ward in her scruffy slippers and down the stairs to have a cigarette. She wandered around the whole department, slithering about, casting her scheming predatory eyes on everyone and everything. She spoke with a broad, gruff regional accent, as though her voice had been ripped out of the ground and hewn from a rough lump of local rock. Every other word was 'fuck'. If she'd done a little less of that word, or at least been more careful, she wouldn't be in that place, in that condition, at all.

I took as many statements as I could. Staff, as usual, were very helpful. They put me in contact with other patients, since discharged, who had indicated they had items missing, but who had not yet, for whatever reason, contacted the police. There were fourteen victims in all. I managed to trace them and take statements from them all. At some point or another, during their stay, Lara had been up to their beds and befriended them and sat on, or by their beds. While I was making enquiries in the ward, Lara must have seen my uniform and realised why I'd been called. She discharged herself and left. She'd not yet had her baby, but had been in for a check following a brief scare. She was actually due in three weeks' time. Curiously, once she'd left the building, I found out more about this young woman, from staff and patients suddenly more willing to speak to me. One of the maternity nurses had found her in the staff rest room on the ward, very late, on the first night of her two-day stay, with her hands actually inside a nurses hand bag. The nurse, Mary, challenged her immediately. Lara simply walked up to Mary and without hesitation or provocation, head-butted her as hard as she could. This was obviously accompanied by a wildly recalcitrant plethora of very loud 'fucks', before she just wandered casually back to her bed, as though nothing had happened.

Mary hadn't reported this assault to the police but merely completed a hospital 'incident report'. So many hospital staff seem to accept assault, both verbal and physical, as somehow being part of their job. Such an assault on medical staff would not look good for Lara in court to say the least. So we paid her a visit at home. We searched her obnoxious place of abode thoroughly. Despite the usual rancid smell, and having to wade ankle-deep through the dirt and filth inside the place, we found dozens of credit cards. And drugs, of course. As I've said before, finding stolen items in a person's home address is the very best evidence. She admitted fourteen thefts in the maternity department in those brief two days. I submitted the evidence and awaited a charging decision. Meanwhile, I was in receipt of frequent updates from many of the victims. Lara had been travelling into the city centre with various items stolen from the other pregnant ladies and used their identity documents to open store cards, which she then used to the maximum on each occasion. The first thing the victims knew were letters arriving from the stores stating 'Welcome to our store! The balance on your new card is now £750 debit. Thank you for opening an account with us!' Obviously the ladies did not wish to pay these debts, understandably, and I had to help them all by providing proof they had been victims of identity theft. Several of these ladies were even informed their credit ratings had been undermined by this episode, despite my best efforts to help them. The new modern crime of 'identity theft'. It is a very distressing experience for those who are victims of it and it can have far-reaching consequences. A number of these ladies were in tears they were so upset at what had happened. Having a baby should have been a wonderful, beautiful experience. Their precious moments were forever tarnished by the acts of this selfish, invidious woman. But Lara wasn't bothered. Not in the least. She couldn't care less. She wanted what she wanted and that was that.

I rang her solicitor when I had the charging decision, almost a month later. She was to get nine charges, including the assault on the nurse, Mary, and the remaining offences were to be 'Taken into Consideration'. Her solicitor informed me Lara was actually in maternity that day and was due to have her baby. He stated she was in no position to see me. Okay, I thought, I'll bear that in mind. 'I'll see you there in ten minutes then,' I said to him, putting the phone down. I asked which ward she was in this time, as I arrived at maternity reception. 'Oh, she's in the labour suite. She's having the baby,' I was told. I didn't knock. I just swiped and walked in. She was lying on her back, propped up, her legs slung high up, wide open, in the stirrups, while drawing on gas and air. It was a case of 'head visible' too, apparently, though I didn't look that close myself! To a small crowd of astonished hospital staff I read the charges to Lara, one by one. I wrote 'refused to sign' on the triplicate copies, and tore off hers, leaving it on the bed. 'Thanks!' I shouted, over her groans and moans, and left. When she finally appeared in Crown Court she was sent to prison for a year. She served six months. I've not heard anything of her since. No doubt if she still lives in my city, someone, some day, may cause themselves to be suitably inebriated enough to have sex with her, and she'll be back in maternity!

ORBS

I'd never heard of 'orbs' before. I didn't know anything about them. You may not know anything about them either, as you read this. They are, as far as I understand and has been explained to me, the spirits of dead people. The 'orb' itself is a circle of light, like a ball, floating in the air, and is usually best seen in photographs. You can see them in quite a few photographs. You may have some yourself, but are so far unaware of them. Shaun, the security guard, told me about them. Shaun is a person who you would describe, if you met him, as a genuinely 'nice bloke'. A thoroughly decent chap. Always helpful, outgoing and positive, yet on occasions strangely diffident and reserved. He used to live in a small house in a street built on land which was once a mortuary, near the back of the hospital. He showed me numerous photographs of his family in their living room. There were orbs everywhere in these pictures. Large ones, small ones, groups of orbs together, on the floor, on the walls and in the air, just floating.

One afternoon we were discussing this phenomenon in the security office. Shaun had brought these photos into work for us to examine as evidence. Clearly they were there in the pictures. The orbs. Nigel, always the pragmatist, stated they were dust particles either in the room at the time, and reflected at the moment the photo was taken, or specks on the lens. If that was the case, then there was a lot of dust about! Would that explain other occasions when there were no orbs, or dust, in any photographs? Apparently the same camera had been used to take pictures in Shaun's new house, miles away from the hospital, where not a single orb had been found in any photographs. Not only this, a colleague of Shaun's, Julie, had borrowed Shaun's camera to take on holiday. No orbs have ever been revealed in any of Julie's holiday snaps. I'm afraid we had a laugh at Shaun's expense though, as Nigel made photocopies of some of Shaun's photos and drew smiley faces in the orbs. But as always, I maintain an open mind about it. The orbs, that is, not the smiley faces!

The new car park across from the back of the maternity building was once an old red brick nurses' accommodation. It had been empty and boarded up for ten years or more. I was told it was one of the first such old buildings to have been abandoned. Shaun told me this. He also told me it was due to the orbs and other paranormal phenomenon. In essence, the main reason the building was abandoned is that no-one was willing to live in it any longer, it was so haunted. So many times, apparently, nurses had complained of wailing and moaning in the night. Footsteps along the dark corridors which stopped outside rooms, followed by tapping on the doors. There was never anyone there when these sounds were investigated, and they just seemed to get worse. Door handles were rattled frantically and noisily, causing loss of sleep and an eventual exodus of residents from the building. On one occasion, Shaun recalled, he was caught short and needed to use one of the toilet cubicles in the building. While he sat on a toilet in the middle cubicle, he heard someone approaching, along the corridor. The footsteps grew louder until they eventually came into the room. They stopped directly outside the door to the cubicle. Shaun's first thought was someone was actually wanting to use the very toilet he was sitting on, and so was initially quite vexed that this should happen. Why didn't they use one of the adjacent cubicles? The person wasn't saying anything, so Shaun opened the door quickly, to confront this person. Of course, there was no-one there.

Shaun was asked to investigate just such an incident one night, with a colleague, long after all the residents had left. As in other similar calls, it was thought local kids had gained entry to the building by pulling the boards from the windows. But as they drew up in their van they could see that there did not appear to be any insecurity. In fact, a cursory check around the outside revealed it to be completely intact and secure. Shaun unlocked the main doors and walked in, torch in hand.

I would guess that walking into a building such as this, knowing its reputation as he did, in the dark (it had to be dark didn't it?!) Shaun was probably already a little on edge, to say the least. But undeterred he stepped inside with Tony, his colleague, behind him. They walked along the main corridor on the ground floor. It was a calm night with no wind. So what happened next caused them to assume kids were in the building after all. Ten yards ahead of them, a light bulb flew across the corridor from one open empty room into another, across and in front of them, and smashed on the floor in the room ahead and to their left. They walked straight into the room where the bulb had come from and shone their torches around all four walls, fully expecting to see at least one giggling teenager. Nothing. No-one there. The ceiling light was hanging there, swinging gently, minus a bulb. Across the corridor the remains of the bulb were littered around the floor. Shards of broken bulb glittered and sparkled in

Shaun's torchlight. A breeze apparently then started blowing down the corridor, gently at first, but then inexplicably strong, swirling around the two men. Apparently icy cold, despite the fact it was a warm night. At that moment both men state they heard someone whispering to them in the churchy darkness, though not from a distance, but right up close, directly into their ears. Multiple layered voices in a hurried and peremptory tone, though they couldn't quite understand what was being said to them.

Shaun reached for his phone, not to make a call, but to take a photograph. He has stated he amazed himself at the level of composure it took him to do this, as he fumbled in the torchlight to prepare his phone for camera mode. He took a single photograph of Tony standing there in the corridor, in his yellow coat, at the open doorways where the light bulb had flown across their path. There are orbs everywhere in this photograph. They were behind Tony, over his shoulder, and gathered around him in a group, as though curious and wanting to see and be seen.

I've seen this photo, and Shaun's other photos. I've looked on the internet for orbs. Have a look yourself. You'll have to decide what you think about them. The building I've just described no longer exists. It's a very smart new car park. Before it was demolished Shaun never once ventured inside again. At least not on his own!

CAR CRIME

A tale of a hospital cannot be complete without some more auto-crime, as we call it. We had our fair share of this blight at our hospital. With some fifteen thousand vehicle movements a day and car parking for around five thousand cars in more than thirty-five formal car parks, it's not really surprising. I remember one summer afternoon strolling along South Road among the conker trees, being interrupted in my thoughts by a chap who came running up to me, in a very distressed state, shouting, 'Officer, officer, my car, my car!' His car had been broken into, badly damaged and an overnight bag taken from the back seat. He was staying near the hospital in a hotel, or at least had planned to, as he lived several hours drive away. His elderly father had just had both legs amputated, only that very afternoon. Bad news and traumatic enough. Now someone had forced their way into his car and taken his belongings. I felt real sympathy for this man and remember looking around me in a vain attempt to see if I could find anyone, at that moment, acting suspiciously around vehicles: As though I had an immediate obligation to be seen acting policeman-like. But I knew at the time that this was not an isolated, random incident. There were several others that day. Security and I were on the lookout for a particular car, with a particular registration number. But it never seemed to come on the campus more than once or twice. Then another vehicle would be seen on the CCTV apparently patrolling the car parks, in the same manner, suspiciously pausing at vehicles before being driven away. It seemed as though the hospital was being targeted by a group of offenders using many different vehicles. We could never have guessed what was really happening.

Scanning the CCTV cameras we found a common thread through all of these particular incidents. A middle-aged chap with a beer-belly, thick beard, and bald head. He seemed to be in most of the cars seen cruising the campus. One day he'd be in a particular car, with a certain number plate, then another car which looked like the same, or similar vehicle, but with an entirely different number plate. It was very confusing and quite difficult to keep track of. But it was always the same man, plus one other, in the cars.

I took the best photo we had of this man from the hospital and submitted it into our intelligence database at the police station. It was published across the police intranet, force-wide. Then to surrounding forces, with a plea from me asking whether anyone knew who he was. Casting a net as wide as this I eventually had an answer. I didn't just get his identity, but the man himself. I came on duty one morning and was told immediately by the control room to contact the main custody suite in the city. Daniel James Ross, he of the beard and bald head, had been arrested in a car making off from the scene of an auto-crime offence in the car park of a large hotel in the city centre in the early hours. Colleagues in another part of the city were also evidently after this same man. I gathered up all my papers relating to around twenty or so cases of auto-crime at the hospital and went to see him.

Queuing in the custody suite is nothing new or unusual. It can be a very busy place. It takes a while to book someone in. Lots of questions about their physical and mental state, their history and even their diet, in order to ensure their safe passage while in police custody. But this was a different kind of queue. I had to wait my turn to speak to this man due to the fact that so many of my colleagues also wanted to speak to him! I'd never quite known a prisoner to be so popular among so many colleagues across my force area. It didn't stop there, either. Once he'd been identified, no less than five other regional police forces also wanted him! It seemed he'd been breaking into cars on a vast, industrial scale for months. So how did he do it? How had he not been caught before now?

When I questioned him he was predictably tight-lipped and had decided to say 'No Comment' to all questions. But I had some good quality CCTV in my possession, which he didn't know about, so I wasn't worried. You let them dig themselves into a hole, before producing your best hand. Get them to deny being at the scene, deny any knowledge, or continue to give no explanation, by way of the no comment replies. Then go for the throat. I showed him the photos and played him the CCTV. He then started talking to me. 'That's just a picture of me standing at a car,' he said when I showed him the stills. His solicitor was clearly getting agitated and kept telling him to be quiet. Then I showed him moving CCTV images of him in south car park, actually breaking into a car. This was the same car park the chap ran up to me about, whose father had both legs amputated, though not the same car. It was a brilliant recording. The camera was some distance away on the roof of haematology and had clearly, and irrefutably, caught everything. He'd obviously not seen this camera. His face dropped. He looked at his solicitor and mumbled something to him. His solicitor, a pale, sullen looking thin-faced man, peering over bi-focal spectacles, then asked for a private consultation.

An hour later we resumed the interview. He admitted breaking into two cars in south car park. One in north and one in maternity car park. I knew he'd done at least twenty on the campus, but that was all I had evidence for, so that was all he would admit. It happens like that.

While I'd been interviewing Mr Ross, colleagues had been searching his home address. It soon became clear as to how he'd managed to evade capture and commit so much crime. He had access to four vehicles but a limitless number of registration plates. He had a number plate making machine in his garage. It was no problem therefore, for him to see a car of a certain type, produce his own registration plate and drive around, frequently changing it whenever he wanted. Three of the four cars he had access to were in fact stolen. It was a professional operation, like a small business, with staff, helpers and employees. He eventually went to prison for four years.

Our other prolific auto-criminal was Jake Godfrey. He lived in the estate across the main road. Not part of my beat area. A socially challenged, uninteresting lad, twenty years of age, he would play on his Playstation and smoke cannabis until three in the morning when he'd then decide, with a mate, or on his own, to wander onto the campus and commit crime. He had little or no formal structure to his life and was not in any education, employment or training. He was literally wasting his life away. He didn't seem to know, or care, about the cameras on the hospital campus either. He would always be seen to wander on site, making no efforts to hide his identity. At first we didn't know who he was. But I put out an ad on our intelligence system, as I'd done with Ross, and a colleague soon contacted me, having recently dealt with him. One particular night he strolled into the hospital via south entrance and walked around all of the car parks. He'd broken into no less than nine cars before being spotted lurking in the shadows and police were called. He jumped into one of the cars, managed to get it started, and led the police on a chase into the city centre. He crashed it, unfortunately not causing himself any injury, or anyone else, luckily, and was locked up for the night. This was the only time he was locked up for his crimes, as when he finally appeared at court he was given a suspended sentence. And he was banned from ever re-entering the hospital!

MOTORBIKES

North Road curves gently around the back of maternity, one side of which backs straight onto the fence dividing the campus from the nearby council housing estate. There's a small staff car park around the back with thick brambles growing wild and unfettered on the land around it. In summer these are heavy and resplendent with huge plump blackberries, which sadly no-one ever seems interested in. I've stood there, occasionally, in full uniform, picking and eating some of these plump fruits, no doubt being watched from the many windows overlooking the car park. I would always try to remind myself to return with jam-jars and a plain coat to pick as many as I could. But as with so many 'notes to self', once out of sight, the idea is quickly forgotten, lost among so many other, more important thoughts. This car park lies lower down than the road around it and the brambles obscure anyone standing in it from view of the road. Above that, the fence. Behind the fence, a long straight footpath. This was once a railway line. Used in the First World War to bring casualties to the hospital. Unfortunate men with horrific injuries. Many of these soldiers were brought in with chest injuries and lung damage from gas inhalation. Huge numbers died in the various wards. The hospital has since developed as one of the best chest-lung centres in the country.

The path runs the entire length of the hospital fence on the north edge. It was on this path that I saw big fat Mick

McGough riding a motorbike, one warm summer Sunday afternoon. Maternity staff had been complaining of a very noisy motorbike being ridden along this path, mainly at weekends. It was always the quietest of days too. As though these people on these noisy machines take the greatest pleasure in creating their noise nuisance to annoy, on only the quiet days, to maximum effect. Rarely do they ever ride around on cold, blustery, rainy days. I was walking along North Road near maternity when I heard the machine approach. Very loud and sounding as though it was coming from some enormous motorcycle, or even something the size of a tractor. I looked up to my left through the fence as the machine sped past on the path.

Mick McGough, at that time, probably weighed in excess of twenty stone. He was, and as far as I know, still is, a huge lad. He was twenty-four at that time, and from the conversations I'd had with him, he didn't seem to have a great deal going on between his ears. Despite also being very tall, well over six foot, and commanding a certain obvious presence, he was surprisingly timorous and unthreatening in his manner. But then I'd not really fallen out with him yet. As the bike sped past, my first thoughts were how he could actually manage to ride the particular machine he was on. He looked, at that moment, as though he could easily have been profitably employed in a circus. He was riding what has been variously described as a 'monkey bike', a very small motorcycle, with wheels no bigger than around twelve inches in diameter. Probably about thirty cc engine size, and tiny handlebars. The engine was obviously screaming in agony with the weight of its rider but despite this, astonishingly it was making a good thirty miles an hour along the path. At first glance the machine wasn't even visible under Mick's vast bulk.

His legs were thick and flabby and his backside was hanging over the seat in a type of Daliesque manner, his great folds of flesh smothering everything he was sitting on. I was surprised part of him wasn't in direct contact with the hot engine and therefore slowly cooking as a result. Maybe it was! He was showing some huge backside cleavage too, replete with thick black hair and spots.

In the instant he passed me, as I stood thirty feet away on North Road, he turned his head and looked perfectly sideways, at ninety degrees, straight at me. A huge bulk, with tiny wheels underneath, travelling from right to left at high speed, with a human head on the top, eyes as wide as dinner plates when they saw me. His big, round, red face turned back to the front again and he disappeared behind some trees. I expected to hear a loud crashing sound accompanied by shrieks of pain and clattering about, but I just heard the machine fade away, then stop. Then it grew louder again as it was clearly being ridden back in my direction. Surely he wouldn't be daft enough to ride past me again? But he did. As he grew closer I scrambled up to the fence to take a closer look. He rode the machine on a stretch of road between two blocks of flats, narrowly missing several parked cars, before mounting the kerb and back onto the path. This time as he rode by, I could have almost reached out and touched him. He looked panicked, as though his first sight of me had been an apparition that hadn't really happened. There was no doubting this time though. The bike, and Mick, passed me in clouds of oily exhaust smoke and sped off along the path, again at high speed. The path is in constant use by pedestrians, old and young alike, and anyone stepping into it in the way of this motorized monster would have met with certain serious injury, or even death. There were no lights, indicators, registration plates, road tax, in fact nothing at all that would make the riding of the bike anywhere near legal. It would be unlikely, therefore, that there was any insurance. I wasn't sure if he had a driving licence of any sort at that time either. I knew where Mick lived, on my estate, so I went to see him.

I'd met his mother, Pamela, before. I'd previously dealt with his sister, a rather strange teenage hoyden by the name of Gemma, on a few occasions, but nothing particularly serious. Mainly anti-social behaviour and general nuisance matters. But all my visits to their house were greeted with masses of unwarranted vitriolic abuse, even when bringing them good news. So I was prepared for what happened when I arrived at their door. I've provided a translation, in order to help understand the conversation:

"Hello, Pamela, how are you?"

"What the fuck's it got to do with you?" ("I'm fine, officer, how are you?") and then:

"What you doin' 'ere anyway? What do your fuckin' lot want?" ("What can I do for you, how may I be of assistance to the police?")

Despite standing on her doorstep completely alone, I was obviously 'the police', plural, 'your lot', and therefore a representative of the oppressive and vindictive law-enforcement authority, which she obviously loathed.

"Is your Mick in at the moment?"

"You can fuck off, Mick's done nowt!" (I'm not sure officer, I'll find out for you.")

You may be forgiven for thinking at this point that I wasn't welcome, I'd been told to go away, and that I was wasting my time. But no. Not entirely. I know these particular people, and this is in fact just how they converse with one another, all the time. In this instance, for example, 'fuck off' actually means something like 'Oh alright, just a moment,' or similar.

She turned and screamed like a banshee up the stairs behind her:

"Mick! Fuckin' coppers are 'ere! What you bin fuckin' up to?" ("Mick, there's a police officer to see you, would you mind coming down to speak to him?")

The top of the stairs darkened as Mick's vast bulk padded slowly downwards towards me, causing each step to groan and creak as he descended.

"Could I come in a minute and have a chat to you?" I said, optimistically lifting a foot onto their step.

Pamela, still standing at the door, scowled at me scathingly as though I'd just asked her a highly impertinent, personal question.

"No you fuckin' can't. No copper's comin' in my 'ouse!" (I'm sorry officer, it's a bit inconvenient at the moment, so I'd rather not, if that's okay with you.")

"Okay then, I'll have to do it here, on the doorstep," I said, taking out my pocket book.

"Do what here? What the fuck you on about?" ("What's this all about, anyway officer?")

Pamela stood defiantly at the door, one hand on it, gripped tightly, as though guarding a roomful of priceless artefacts, instead of a scruffy carpet-less cave, with a tired old three-piece, and the world's largest television.

I carried on. On the doorstep:

"Mick. Have you got a driving licence?"

"No he fuckin' hasn't, why?" ("I don't think he does, officer.") Pamela was very insistent, and obviously very protective of her loving son.

I cautioned Mick, in the usual way, as I suspected him

of several traffic offences, to be again greeted with expressions of concern and derision, in equal measure, from Pamela:

"What the FUCK are you on about?" ("What's the problem officer?")

Both were standing in the doorway, each jostling the other to get a view of what I was writing. Pamela was almost the same size as her son but, sadly for her, with more hair on her chin and so even less attractive.

I persisted:

"Mick, have you got a driving licence, insurance, and MOT certificate for the motorbike I saw you riding earlier today?" Pamela threw an angry glance at her son, then back at me:

"What fuckin' motorbike? He 'ant got a fuckin' motor bike! You're fuckin' well wrong there. Oh no, you're fuckin' wrong there! Tell him Mick!"

Mick didn't say anything. He looked at his mother, then back at me, then at the floor. I asked another question:

"Where is the motorbike I saw you riding earlier today?"

At last he spoke for himself, before his mother could give me a reply:

"It's not mine. It's not here. It's a mate's."

Thanks Mick. I'll put that comment in my pocket book.

"So you admit riding the motorbike this morning at the back of the hospital?"

Pamela took hold of her son and tried to push him back towards the stairs.

"No he fuckin' doesn't!" and slammed the door in my face. Undeterred I continued talking to them both through the letter box:

"Mick, I'm reporting you for the offences of riding a motorcycle without a licence, insurance, registration plates and MOT. Oh, and for not wearing a helmet. Do you understand?"

I listened at the door for any sort of reply. I heard some scuffling, some chuntering, loud swearing, and I then heard Pamela's voice again, in a very loud shriek, by way of reply, and on behalf of her son, out the letter-box:

"FUCK OFF!"

I returned to the station and completed my pocket book, pretty much the same as what's written above. I filled in the necessary forms and eventually Mick was summonsed to court. He was, not surprisingly, pleading not guilty. In court, he did not have any legal representation. The biggest reason for this is, at that time anyway, Legal Aid was not available for what were purely traffic related offences. In fact there was no-one else in court with him at all. Not even his curmudgeonly mother. So it was that I was the only witness for the prosecution and he was the only defence witness. This would be interesting! There was no CCTV, as the hospital cameras didn't reach the other side of the fence. So, as is procedure, as the prosecution, I gave my evidence first. I recounted the story as described above. I could see the three magistrates' eyebrows rising occasionally as they wrote some notes on their papers in front of them. The court clerk asked Mick if he wanted to challenge any of my evidence. He just stood up and said to the clerk, in an inappropriately bellowing voice, which echoed around the near-empty court room:

"It weren't me." Then flopped back down in his seat.

The clerk told me I was released, and could either go, or sit at the back of the court. I found a discreet chair near the main doors. I wanted to hear Mick's defence. Maybe he'd found a witness willing to lie for him? Had he fabricated some far-fetched and clever excuse or alibi, placing him a hundred miles away at the time that I said I'd seen him? I was very curious to find out what he was up to. The court clerk invited him to speak. He stood up to start his defence:

"It weren't me," he said, again. Then sat down, with a heavy thump onto his chair and stared into space.

The clerk looked embarrassed. He briefly turned to the magistrates, than back at Mick:

"Is that it, Mr McGough?"

Mick looked at him and, without standing or looking at the bench, replied:

"Yeah."

The magistrates could see I was still in the room. It didn't take them long to pass judgement.They didn't even bother to retire to their room for a chat. It came down to simple facts, and who was the more believable. An experienced police officer with a quarter of a century of service, or him. I am pleased to say, not to mention relieved, he was found guilty, given six penalty points on a licence he didn't yet have and was fined three hundred pounds.

DOMESTIC VIOLENCE

Past maternity, North Road straightens out and stretches all the way, over half a mile, back to the entrance I usually use, as described at the start of this book. At night it looks quite pretty, as there are no less than five pedestrian crossings along North Road. The amber globes of the Belisha beacons flash inordinately and out of time to one another, constantly, all through day and night. There are some tall new blocks of doctors' accommodation on the left and across the road the back of the sterile services buildings. Adjacent to these are the operating theatres. I've been inside these areas a few times; known as 'green areas', because everyone in the theatres has to wear the green sterile clothing. I had a job there once. Well, the person I had to see had been in theatres for some time when I was told about her. I had to wait a few days until she was safely ensconced in a bed in a nearby ward before I could actually see her. Amanda Rushley had been the victim of domestic violence, along with her infant son. The phrase 'domestic violence' can mean anything, of course, from psychological and financial bullying, smoothed over by the occasional perfunctory embrace, right across the spectrum of violence to rape and murder. So it can sometimes be a euphemism for very serious crime. As in this case.

Amanda had been enjoying an afternoon at home with her ten-month old son Zak. They lived in a generally rough part of town, but Amanda was determined to make a positive difference to her life and bring up her son to the very best of her abilities. Zak was up to date with all of his vaccinations, and the health visitor came to see them regularly. He was putting on weight and was healthy. Amanda herself had something of a chequered past and had kept some very unpleasant company until recently. That included the baby's father, Eric Jeremy Bethell. He was in prison, but was due to come out soon, as far as Amanda was aware. She hadn't wanted anything more to do with him. He was serving an eighteen-month term for supplying Class A drugs. But after only nine months he was due for release. The baby was his, though he'd not yet seen him, and Amanda did not *want* him to see Zak, or be part of their lives in any way for that matter. She knew what he was like and knew what he was capable of. He frightened her. The last nine months had been a blissful respite from his unwarranted attentions. Zak's very conception virtually amounted to rape, under normal circumstances, but she hadn't reported it due to fear of repercussions from Eric. She was in a desperate situation and was just pleased to be rid of him. But then he was released.

Amanda and Zak had moved since Eric was imprisoned, but not far enough away. She still lived in the same neighbourhood. Friends knew where she lived, and some of these friends were mutual to both herself and Eric. She shopped in the same mini-markets and occasionally went in the same pubs. She was kidding herself if she thought Eric wouldn't find her. And he did. Zak had just fallen asleep for his afternoon nap when Amanda had sat down to enjoy a quiet cup of tea. An old black-and-white film was on the television and she loved old movies, so she hoped Zak would sleep long enough for her to watch at least some of it in peace. She'd taken a few sips of her tea when there was the most almighty bang from the rear of the house. There was a sound like the ripping of wood and metal, and several short, sharp stamping noises. Amanda immediately felt sick to her stomach. She instinctively knew what this meant and who it was. She grabbed hold of Zak from where he was sleeping in his chair and bolted for the front door.

The next five minutes of her life she told me later, were as if she had dreamt them, or had been experiencing in a living nightmare. Worse than any Hollywood horror. She states that she remembered she reached the front door, but it was locked. As she tried to unlock it, valuable, life-changing seconds were lost. The first thing she remembers was being grabbed by the hair from behind and pulled to the floor, viciously, and in one quick, irresistible movement. Still with Zak in her arms she heard loud banging noises accompanied by searing pain and couldn't initially work out what they were. Then she realised she was being struck on the head, over and over again. In fact, Eric was kicking her head as she lay there on the floor, trying to curl up into a foetal position, mainly in an effort to protect Zak. The kicks moved around as Eric started kicking her about the body, seemingly with all the strength he could muster. With an impossible amount of effort, Amanda managed to get up almost to her knees and started screaming and shouting. She then saw it was indeed Eric. His face was distorted and fierce with apoplectic rage, and she could smell beer and cigarettes on his breath. She states she cried out: "Eric, please!" but he didn't say anything at all. He then took hold of Zak by the legs and ripped him away from his mother. Without a pause for thought, but with clear, deliberate intent, he swung the baby around by the legs and threw him hard against the far wall of the living room. The poor little lad struck the wall and dropped with a thud onto the floor. There was no crying from him. Nothing.

Amanda now thought she was going to be killed. She had nothing to lose, so she began to kick and punch at Eric, screaming as she did so. But Eric was bigger, stronger and a far more experienced fighter of women. It's precisely what he enjoyed doing the most when he'd had ten pints of lager. He thoroughly enjoyed beating women, as they could never hit him back as hard as he could hit them. The few occasions he'd picked a fight with a man in the past, particularly coppers, they'd always hit him back a lot harder and he'd lost the battle. But women were easy. Not only this, he enjoyed hearing them beg for mercy; it made him feel such a thrill of power, such a rush, a feeling that otherwise was completely absent in every other aspect of his life. He could already sense he'd got the upper hand with Amanda, so began to take his time a little, to savour these precious moments. He'd waited a long time for this. He would make sure she would not disrespect him again. He managed two straight arm punches to Amanda's face almost immediately. Her nose burst open in an explosion of blood and mucus, spattering the wall, and her cheekbones ripped and contused. Again he hit her, harder and harder, on her face, over and over. She states she actually remembers thinking at the time, 'Why doesn't he say something?' as the pummelling continued. But he didn't, he just carried on, without saying a word. She was backed up against the front door and beaten and punched about the face and body in an occasionally ferocious, frenzied manner, then calmly, as though he was physically tiring. Which of course he was. Try maintaining a series of blows on a punch-bag in the gym, you'll find it soon becomes very exhausting. Every time she tried to move, another blow struck her somewhere. She just couldn't get away. She could feel her knees slowly giving way under her, as she started to slide down the wall next to the door. She began to feel nauseous and light-headed and felt herself drifting into unconsciousness. By now she wasn't too bothered anyway. He'd won. She was obviously going to die.

Suddenly it stopped. After what had seemed hours, but was only a few minutes, she was left alone. Still barely conscious, she sat slumped on the floor, near the door. Her tormentor walked calmly into the kitchen and out of sight. Should she rest there and gather some strength to try to fight back if he returned? What should she do? And where was Zak? She looked across the room. She could only see with her left eye. Something was wrong with her right eye. It felt like it was full of warm water and she felt something dripping, almost pouring onto her clothes. It was blood. She couldn't breathe through her nose and she felt several teeth were loose. The sweet, sickly taste of blood was filling her mouth. The next sound that came from the kitchen told her, that at whatever cost, however she did it, she must get out of the house, now. She heard the kitchen draw being pulled open and Eric was rifling through the cutlery drawer.

Amanda crawled across the floor and found Zak adjacent to the sofa, apparently lifeless. His head had made the first contact with the wall and had broken open like a melon. There was a huge amount of blood. She crawled back to the door, dragging Zak by one arm, as best she could. The key was in the lock. She reached up, in a gargantuan effort, all the time trying her very best to be as quiet as she possibly could. Without looking back, the key turned sweetly and smoothly in the lock and she opened the door. Just for a second she feared another grab from behind. But it never came. She fell down a single step into the street. With energy summoned from the very depths of her soul, she stood up and ran down the road. She started screaming. She screamed a primal, atavistic scream, desperate for someone, anyone to hear her. She didn't know what to do, or where to go, so she just started banging on as many doors as she could, all down the street. She was trying to make as much noise as she possibly could.

The first poor chap to open his front door thought Amanda had been in some horrific car accident. Her face was smashed open and swollen like he'd never seen a human face before. He also thought this desperate woman was holding a large piece of fresh meat in her arms, until he realised it was in fact a baby. Both were soaked in blood and there was blood continuing to flow from rips and tears apparently from all over their bodies.

Luckily police had been called a few minutes earlier, neighbours having heard the screaming and arrived on the scene very quickly. Eric had fled. He didn't want to hang around for the coppers, they might have hurt him. But he was captured a few days later after a serious manhunt by a team of experienced detectives. He was sent back to prison. He'd only been out a day.

There was a huge and comprehensive list of injuries to both Amanda and Zak. I included them all in the statement I took from Amanda as I sat by her hospital bed. I read them from her patients' notes, but also included the doctor's reports as exhibits. Miraculously they both survived. After she'd had extensive reconstructive surgery.

I saw photographs of them both before the incident. Amanda was once a very beautiful woman.

It pretty much happened as I've just described it. A quiet afternoon utterly transformed, and which changed their lives forever. This type of incident is not particularly rare. A huge proportion of murders are domestic-related. Many women are killed by their partners, or ex-partners. Amanda and Zak have changed their identities and moved away. A very long way away.

WEED

Near the theatres, there are several wards which seem to be mainly occupied by elderly patients. People who have had trips and falls, or hip operations, and so on. A bed in one of these wards was frequently occupied by an elderly Jamaican gent called Dennis Isiah Daniels. I'd spoken to him a few times before when I'd encountered him wandering around the nearby corridors in his slippers and dressing-gown. "Maaarnin' afficer!" he'd shout as I'd walk up to him. We'd chat briefly, just to pass a few moments, and he was always complimentary about my shiny boots and smart appearance. He was always full of praise for the hospital staff too: the doctors, the nurses and even the ladies who served him his meals. Dennis was a lovely old chap, sweet-natured and kind. But he was a damned annoying old sod too. He was admitted several times one year, having had a hip replacement and some lung problems. I think his first visit, for his hip, had given him an appetite, a taste, for some more stays in the hospital. It was just too warm and too cosy to turn down! Not unusual, you may say. There are plenty of patients who occupy bed space unnecessarily and quite clearly use the hospital as a convenient, money-saving hotel. But Dennis really was taking liberties. He carried on his habits in the ward, too, he felt so much at home. I don't mean he snored, or broke wind, though apparently he did these too, frequently. I'm talking about his cannabis smoking.

There was a job on the box, on our computer, about a call to this particular ward. A patient, Dennis, was thought to have been smoking cannabis in the ward and trying to blow the smoke out of the window in a crude attempt to avoid detection. Apparently staff had warned him about it frequently, but he continued to persist. The whole thing was made worse due to the fact the entire campus was supposedly 'smoke free'. So smoking anything in the wards was taboo, let alone illegal drugs. So I went to see the offender to put him right.

"Hello, officer, what can I do for you?" Dennis said as he extended a hand. He shook my hand tightly, and vigorously, smiling broadly at me as he did so, with a knowing look, and a glint of familiarity in his eyes.

"Dennis?" I said, peering at him, "Do you remember me?" I said, as I went to sit sideways on his bed.

"Yeah, maaan," he replied, in a long Jamaican drawl. He smiled to reveal a full set of near-perfect white teeth, whiter than the tight ringlets of grey hair in his beard.

"You've been smoking in the ward, Dennis, haven't you?" I said, hoping for an easy response. Dennis' expression changed slightly and he sucked his teeth and leaned his head slightly to one side.

"It's only a bit o' weed, ya know..." he replied, looking around the room, as if seeking approval, and he continued:

"Has someone been ringing the police on me for this? I don't believe it you know. You have better tings to do than deal with likkle tings like this surely, man?" as he sucked air through his teeth again, slightly shaking his head.

"Yes, Dennis, because no-one is allowed to smoke in hospitals any more, not just weed," I said, in a pleading tone, then: "Have you got any left, what have you done with it Dennis?"

He said nothing but reached into the pocket of his pyjamas. He leaned across the bed and handed me a small plastic bag, with a picture of a cannabis plant on it. There were a few crumbs of cannabis still in the bottom.

"That's it you know. That's all. I smoked the rest. It's only a bit o' ganja you know."

He went on to tell me how much of a part of his life cannabis was and, more widely, how much of a cultural influence it has been on Jamaican people. I knew a lot of this of course. In the eighties we used to break up the all-night 'Shabeen' or 'Blues' parties in the city centre flats. The air thick with cannabis smoke and Bob Marley riffs, white police officers finding a cultural void to cross on so many occasions. Sometimes unsuccessfully, and with violent consequences. The ethnic demography now utterly changed of course. These same flats are currently occupied by eastern Europeans and male refugees from Iraq and Afghanistan. More cultural learning curves for the police and other public services.

"Right, Dennis," I said, "I'll have to confiscate this and issue you with a warning."

I took out my 'Cannabis Warning' book of tickets we now use. This has replaced the necessity for arrest in most cases, apart from when the offender is a youngster. I worked my way through the form and noted his replies. Firstly there are questions as to the person's identity and ethnicity. That's two questions about ethnicity. Visual, as seen and judged by the officer, and actual, as stated by the person. They are frequently different! There's space for a brief description of the person and room to put in their PNCID number, if they have one. Standard procedure. Then a warning, obviously aimed at the person filling in the form, that 'Repeat Cannabis Warnings' should not be issued. Then the written thirty-seven word caution. Then the PACE warning. This is a brief warning issued as a result of part of the Police & Criminal Evidence Act 1984, and must be given when in any formal interview situation, if the person is not under arrest: 'You are not under arrest, not obliged to remain with me, and can leave at any time if you wish. Do you understand?' The wording of this warning changes to suit circumstances. If inside someone's home, then it reads 'You have the right to ask me to leave...' If such a warning is issued inside a police station then another, very important line is added: 'You have the right to free legal advice at any time.' This does not apply outside the police station however. If the person decides to exercise their right to ask you to leave, or to leave themselves, as it says in the PACE warning, then there's no problem. You would just arrest them! The questions on the form were as follows:

'Can you please tell me what the substance is I have seized from you?' (Straight in here to get the admission!)

'To whom does the substance belong?' (I've always thought that's much better grammar than simply 'Who's is it?' or 'Who does it belong to?' Obviously devised by an English graduate!)

'Where did you get the substance from?' (A rather pointless question, as no-one has EVER told me where they get their drugs from!)

'What did you intend doing with it?' (Derr... I wonder! But, not quite as daft as it sounds. If the person tells you 'I was going to sell it to a mate,' then you would have possession with intent to supply, a serious offence...)

'How long have you been using cannabis?' (Is this purely a welfare issue, or idle curiosity?)

'Is there anything else you wish to say in relation to this matter?' (This part is the bit where the person says,

'I'm very sorry officer, it won't happen again'. Or more usually, nothing at all.)

There are then some declarations, part of which is the surrendering to the officer of the 'substance'. And lots of room for signatures. Mine, his, and that of my line manager.

Dennis didn't tell me much about anything in his replies. Certainly nothing about where he got it from or anything remotely useful. At the end, he signed for his ticket. I put the cannabis in a small evidence bag and sealed it up.

"Dennis, do NOT do this again in the hospital, do you understand?" I said to him, probably in a vaguely condescending tone.

"Yes okay. I can hear you, you know." And he lay back on his bed, obviously disgruntled and annoyed. He sucked his teeth again. But he still managed a, "Thank you, officer…" at the end, as I left the ward.

We are only supposed to issue such tickets once in twelve months to the same person. No 'repeats', as it clearly stipulates on the form. If a ticket has been issued recently, we are supposed to arrest the offender. The ticket would not result in a conviction, as obviously there is no court appearance. But it does go on a persons' record, if they have one. If they don't already have one, then a police record is created. And a brand new PNCID created. Despite the fact it is dealt with so informally, each incident is issued with a crime number. It is still a crime to be in possession of cannabis. Police officers are now quite relaxed about issuing such forms, as there is little paperwork involved, just the warning form itself, and so if chasing 'detections' they are very quick and easy. I remember a colleague once issued such a form to a student who was carelessly smoking a 'spliff' in the street when a police car drove by. He was issued a cannabis warning form, and that was the end of the matter. A year later, when applying for a job as a teacher, the CRB (Criminal Records Bureau) check revealed a police record for drugs. It caused huge problems for him.

When I returned to the station, I found my ticket to be the third such warning Dennis had been issued in the previous two years! My fault for not checking, I suppose.

POISON

Across the road from these wards are some of the tall new doctors' blocks. Very comfortable one and two bedroom apartments in buildings twelve stories high. Digi-locked and secure, they were built and furnished to a very high standard. The view from the top is superb, from where the whole campus and half the city is visible. I needed access to one of the top-floor rooms to see a doctor who had rung the police to report a particularly strange incident, or series of incidents. I buzzed the room number and introduced myself in the intercom. The door lock clicked and I walked in. Up the stairs to the top floor. No matter how many times I go jogging and no matter how far I walk in the course of my duties, stairs in great numbers such as this have a unique way of quickly tiring me out and reducing me to a breathless, red-faced mess, as though I'd just run a marathon. I stood for a few moments to regain composure, before walking along the hallway to the door. I knocked and heard some movement from within.

Doctor Johannes Schmidt answered the door. A very tall, blonde, Scandinavian doctor, he looked like an athlete for whom any number of stairs would not cause the least concern. He was so well built, and his face so rugged and well-chiselled, at any moment I expected him to ask me for my clothes and my motorcycle.

"Please, come in," he said in a deep voice, and near faultless English, as he eagerly ushered me inside.

"What can I do for you?" I said, leading the way into his living area. I noticed behind me he'd turned the key in the lock as I'd walked away from the door. He was probably very security conscious, or so I thought.

"I'm being poisoned," he said as he stood near his sofa, looking me straight in the eye. I wasn't sure I understood what he meant, or what I'd heard, so I asked him:

"I'm sorry. Did you say you think you are being poisoned?"

"Yes, yes, I am. Someone is trying to poison me. Everything in here has been tampered with, everything. I think someone is definitely trying to poison me."

"Right," I said to him, quickly trying to work out what to say in reply, so I said:

"What makes you think that?"

"Look here, I can show you..." and he led me over to his open-plan kitchen area. He took a tin of cocoa powder from one of the cupboards and removed the lid.

"It's been tampered with. It's got salt in it, look, see?"

"Salt?" I said to him, probably sounding too incredulous to be a concerned professional.

He handed me the tin and I took it, and peered inside. For no reason at all, and similar to when Basil Fawlty opened the briefcase belonging to Lord Melbury, I found myself pointlessly sniffing the contents, as if to detect any salt that may have been fiendishly deposited inside.

"Hmmm..." I said, thoughtfully. Before I could say anything else, he handed me a carton of orange juice from his fridge, quickly removed the lid and said:

"This is the same. It's full of salt. Taste it. You'll find it is full of salt. Someone is doing this to me."

I put down the cocoa tin and took hold of the orange juice. I wasn't about to taste it, so I contented him with a little distracted kind of sniff, not as much as at the cocoa, but enough to play along. He wasn't about to break into laughter and, I soon realised, neither was I. In fact he was deadly serious. There was not a trace of irony anywhere in his face. 'What the *hell* is going on here?' I thought to myself. I made an assumption, for a moment, that what he was telling me was the truth, as he seemed to believe it, so I said:

"Who could be doing this to you, have you any idea?"

"No, no, I've no idea. I have a flat mate, but he's not been here for weeks. No-one else has a key, as far as I know."

"Has anything else happened to you? Have you been burgled, or lost your keys?" I was starting to get a little desperate. What was this man up to? Was he alright?

"No, I have the only keys, but look in here..." he insisted I walk with him down the corridor and into his bathroom. I passed the door which I knew was locked, but I could see the key as still in the lock. I walked after him, and just behind him, into the surprisingly dark bathroom. There was a shower, a toilet and sink, but no outside windows. There were shampoo bottles and aerosols dotted around, as in any other bathroom. He picked up one of the larger bottles of shampoo and handed it to me.

"Open it and look inside. Look at it. Empty some out," his voice peremptory and firm, and seemed to be gaining in urgency as he spoke.

He picked up another bottle and began emptying the contents into the sink, indicating for me to do the same with the bottle in my hand.

"Look!" he said, excitedly. "Look at this!" as pink shampoo, ordinary-looking, thick, pink shampoo drained into the sink and down the plug-hole.

"More salt contamination?" I said, rather sheepishly, desperately searching for a favourable reaction in his face, like when at school, guessing the answer to an impossibly difficult question posed by an unpopular, aggressive science teacher. He certainly did react, but it was not what I had expected:

"No! No! Not salt! Not *salt!* *This* has all been contaminated with *urine*! See, can't you smell it? Someone has put urine in all of these bottles!" he seemed to be getting more agitated by the second. His hands started to shake and he suddenly became physically more jerky and aggressive in his manner.

'Right. That's it,' I thought to myself. 'I'm off. I'm out of here, now.'

"Okay Dr Schmidt. Let me take one of these back to the lab (paraphrasing a hundred fictional tv cop shows) for examination and I'll get back to you, okay?" I made my way towards the door. We were on the top floor don't forget, this chap was a lot bigger than me and he was definitely not quite with us. He seemed to relax a little when I said I was seizing one of the bottles and I said I had to get it to 'the lab' as soon as possible to assist with the enquiry, so any potential evidence was not lost. He unlocked the door and I said my goodbyes.

I only threw the shampoo away a few weeks ago. It sat in my docket at the police station for months. The doctor disappeared. I understand he went back to Sweden. I didn't use any of the shampoo. I didn't fancy the idea of rubbing someone's urine into my hair.

SCRAP

There are quite a few small 'service roads' on the campus which feed vehicular traffic into the areas at the back of many departments. These roads are essential for deliveries, waste collection and so on. There is a huge amount of recycling nowadays, from cardboard and paper, right up to computers and furniture. Of course a good deal of rubbish is generated too, which cannot be recycled, sometimes on the grounds of health and safety. Needles (known as 'sharps') are incinerated, along with other clinical waste. The various bins for these are located in most of the major corridors and outside in the service roads. There are some open, wire mesh, wheeled trolleys in which scrap metal is collected, most of it very bulky and heavy. The hospital has an agreement with some local scrap merchants who are given permission to regularly drive into the campus to collect the metal. But as scrap metal prices have increased, so has the competition to collect it. Unauthorised scrap collectors cruise the campus frequently and have to be ordered off site by security.

The longest service road runs off Franks Way, a road which connects North Road to South Road and runs parallel to Stabbage Way. From Franks Way it looks like two separate roads, but the two meet in the centre of the campus so forming a type of 'U' shape. These are described as Service Road One, and Service Road Two, despite the fact they are connected. It was in Service Road Two where we had some scrap copper piping stolen one night and, again with the help of Nigel and Julie and the rest of the security team, I managed to locate and arrest the offender. Or at least one of them.

A member of staff had arrived at work very early one Monday morning as usual to find a scrap bin he'd filled only the previous Friday night had been completely emptied. The bin was behind tall wooden gates, locked at night. Copper pipe is the best type of scrap and fetches some of the best prices. So I sat with Nigel and we scanned the CCTV in the service roads. Quite quickly we found moving images of two figures late that Sunday night, climbing over the fence into the yard, then standing around the bins, obviously in the process of making their appraisals of the contents, before one of them climbed back over the fence. We then noticed that they had a vehicle parked nearby, a van, with 'County Plumbing Wiring & Heating' written all over it, and clearly visible on the CCTV. So was the vehicle registration number. The man inside the yard passed the copper pipes over the fence to the other one, who slid each pipe one by one into the back of the van. It was all done in only a few minutes.

I rang the company and spoke to their receptionist. I asked to speak to the manager. A female voice came on the line. The wife, and co-director of the family-run business. She apparently took care of the logistics side of the company. She confirmed the van was one of theirs. Employees were allowed to take the vehicles home. This was ironic because if the vans were left in the company yard, they would frequently become the targets for vandals. Despite the firm being thirty miles away I decided to visit in person to speak to the management. I have found that co-operation is gained a good deal quicker, and more readily, when dealing with people in the flesh rather

189

than over the phone, and any ambiguity and formality is soon dispensed with. Clearly one of their staff had been using his company van outside hours for reasons the company would not be entirely happy with! Unless the company themselves were into the scrap recovery business!

Catherine, the Director, was short in stature and round, almost rotund, and her weight seemed impossibly concentrated onto a pair of very thin ankles, at the end of which were two very tiny feet. I followed her into her office, her shoes clickety-clicking on the hard wood floor. The room was spacious and the walls were lined, quite inappropriately I thought, with dark wood panels, floor to ceiling, like some Scottish hunting lodge. A phone on her desk was ringing constantly and Catherine eventually answered:

"Yes, yes, just the stock already ordered, nothing more... make sure, okay?" and abruptly put the phone down.

"Sorry about that. What can I do for you, officer? Something about one of our vans, you mentioned on the phone?" she said, distractedly trying to sort some papers on her desk at the same time.

"This van of yours. Can you tell me who should be driving it at the moment? More importantly, who was driving it over the weekend? Last weekend?"

"Yes, I think I probably can. They don't keep specific vehicles, but we do keep a record of who takes which one. We do allow them to use them at weekends. Within reason, of course." She opened a large folder on her desk and took out a list of names. "Yes here it is. This van has been used by Dave Kilton for the last few weeks. Why, what's the problem?"

"I look after a hospital as part of my duties. This van was seen last weekend being used by two people to steal scrap from the campus."

"Oh. Right. Okay. I see," she said. It was as though she was half expecting this kind of news about this chap, and this van.

"You don't sound too surprised?" I said to her.

"No," she replied. "Dave's activities and behaviour have been a little strange recently." She indicated for me to sit down near her large, very expensive-looking desk.

"Why, what, do you mean?" I said as I pulled at the velcro on my coat and sat down.

"His time-keeping is worse than awful at the moment. His appearance has taken a dive, and he's bumped company vehicles twice in a month. He's missed quite a few days at work with several unlikely-sounding illnesses. Not only that, he seems to be doing way too much mileage at weekends. Unreasonable amounts, I'd say."

"Have you spoken to him about it?"

"Yes, I have. But Dave has been with us since the start. He's been a brilliant member of staff. Malcolm, my husband, keeps telling me to forget about it, to leave him alone, 'It'll be alright' he keeps telling me. Well it won't. And now this! I can tell you now officer, Dave did NOT have our permission to do THAT sort of thing with one of our vehicles!"

I took out some statement paper, tucked inside my stab vest, and began writing. Dave was not authorised to use the vehicle for such activities. It was a straight choice for Catherine and her company. She would either state the vehicle was being used on company business, or it wasn't. If it was, then clearly she and the company were therefore party to the theft at the hospital. If not, then

Dave was using the van without the owners' consent. I took down Dave's home address. He wasn't in work that day. One of his increasingly numerous sick days Catherine had spoken about. Having taken the statement I returned to the hospital. I took another statement from the chap who discovered the scrap missing. It was estimated to have been worth around five hundred pounds.

The next morning Gary and I drove the forty miles to Dave's home address. It was in a nice part of a small town, north of the county. His wife answered the door. She was very polite. And very pretty. The house was an almost new semi-detached, and was very clean inside. We were invited in. Dave was sitting on the sofa.

"I know why you're here. I know. I'm sorry, I've been a bloody idiot."

This sounded very promising! We were not being told to 'f-off', and this chap appeared to be about to tell us something! This was very unusual! I tried to deliberately play down the seriousness and fished for another response:

"Yes, you have. We need to sort it out Dave, don't we?" assuming he was talking about the same incident and the reason I was there.

"Yes I know, I know. I want to get it all sorted out. I'm sick of it and I'm ashamed of what I've been doing."

His wife, Jane, had a baby in her arms, and started crying. Dave stood up, and ran both hands through his hair and shook his head.

"Can we go? I want to get this over with," he said, looking towards the door.

"Where's the copper pipe from the hospital Dave?" I said to him.

"Huh! You're joking aren't you? That's long gone! I never saw anything of it either. Staggy took it all. All I got was one wrap. I've been a bloody fool. I can't believe I've been so stupid!"

Gary searched the back garden and garage while I escorted Dave to the van. He really was one of the most co-operative prisoners I've ever dealt with. We chatted in the van on the forty minute drive back to the station. He told me everything I needed to know. Despite me telling him I'd prefer to start when we arrived at the station, he came forward with an outpouring of confession as though he'd wanted to do this for weeks. In fact he said he had, but hadn't managed to summon up the courage to somehow initiate it for himself. Until then. He didn't have a solicitor in interview. He didn't want one, or need one.

Dave had met a friend of a friend in a pub, about three months before. He'd gone for a drink in one of the more dubious pubs near the hospital after work, having finished a job nearby. A pub with such a bad reputation it no longer exists. It seems unlikely now, but this 'friend' had given Dave some heroin. Dave stated he could not remember how this first came about, other than perhaps he was a thrill-seeker, told people so, and around that time he felt his life was just a little bit boring and, as he stated, could do with a bit of spice. The first time he took it was in the toilets in the pub. It made him ill at first, but Dave and, more importantly, his 'friend' had persisted. Events turned rapidly downwards from then on. Dave was using the company van every weekend for this 'friend'. They seemed to be moving furniture about mostly. Televisions, and boxes of other electrical items. All in return for a wrap or two of heroin. Then came the night he was asked to pick this mate Staggy up near the hospital.

Staggy always met him at the corner, close to the back fence of the hospital. Not far, actually, from Bobby Todd's flat. In fact, the more Staggy was described to me, the more I had my suspicions it could actually have been Todd. Everything about his manner, the location of his flat and lifestyle seemed to fit. But Dave insisted he didn't know his full name and had never been in his flat. That night they'd been in the pub as usual and Staggy suddenly stood up and told Dave to bring the van around to the front. Dave wasn't sure where he was told to drive the van, though he did remember it was some sort of hospital grounds. It was Staggy who climbed the fence and passed the copper pipes over to Dave, who then stacked it all in the van. They drove around the corner and pulled up outside some flats at the back of the hospital. As they pulled up, three other men suddenly appeared from nowhere and took the copper away. In a few seconds it was all gone. Dave was handed a wrap of heroin, and Staggy disappeared into the shadows. Dave drove away, but parked his van in the grounds of a large park, close to his home address and took the heroin, burning it on a spoon. He fell asleep in the van and woke the next morning. He missed work again. He had little clear memory of that previous night, as with the other such nights spent in contact with Staggy.

I charged Dave with TWOC (Taking Without Consent) of the company van and theft of the copper from the hospital. He was fined, and given the usual criminal record. He was sacked from the company too. Gross misconduct. I have since found out he has reformed himself and is back at the same company, having recovered from his brief experiences and venture into drug sub-culture. He was very lucky.

MISSING

Close to the ward in which old Dennis Daniels usually resides in, off North corridor, is an upstairs ward which used to be the Emergency Admissions Unit, the E.A.U. Since E.A.U. moved down to south side, it's since been renamed. It was in this ward that I dealt with another lady who disappeared. Though very real, and made of flesh and bone, this other vanishing lady may very well be as ghostly as the other one on the stairs. Lin Su Din was a Vietnamese lady who was in the hospital following a minor urinary infection. She'd been admitted after referral from another hospital. She'd obviously been in great pain, otherwise she would not have bothered. I can describe exactly what possessions she had with her when she was admitted to the ward. I know she had a plastic carrier bag containing an unopened packet of 'McVities' chocolate digestive biscuits. I know she also had a spare pair of red shoes in this bag, a small towel, a change of underwear, a coat, and a tin of pineapple chunks, unopened. I know she had all these items with her because they are still sitting in our property store at the police station. Why on earth is that? I hear you say. Or maybe not. Well, she was not an invisible spirit, a lost soul wandering the campus. Far from it.

Ms Din had been in the ward for one night. It had been particularly busy and staff hadn't quite managed to get to speak to her in any depth until the first morning. She'd received some initial treatment, including antibiotics and so on when she'd arrived in the late afternoon, the day before, but was due to see a doctor that morning. Ward staff needed to know something of her history before she was treated. Similar, I would imagine, to questions asked by the police when a person is taken into their custody. Personal questions about health, both physical and mental, background, family and so on. Ms Din was struggling with her English, so it was not easy to obtain any of the required information. Add to this her apparently very introverted, placid demeanour, and staff therefore found it extremely difficult to extract anything useful from her at all. As is standard procedure for someone who is obviously not an EU national, she was asked about her immigration status. This was the start of all the trouble. She indicated she needed the toilet and left her bed. She walked out of the ward and didn't return. She was dressed, but made no effort to take her bag of belongings with her.

This was the start of an enquiry which is still running to this day. The problem is of course, if a person is in the care and custody of a hospital, then upon them falls a duty of care for this person while a patient. This person was not formally discharged, and so was, strictly speaking, still in their care. Consequently, if the person disappears, as in this case, then they are classed as 'missing'. So it was that when I arrived on the ward I found her little bag containing all her worldly possessions, hurriedly abandoned on the floor. There was nothing else by the bed. In fact, Ms Din hadn't even made the bed appear slept in, she'd been so careful in the sheets. There were no identity documents left behind. I asked the staff if they'd seen anything by way of passport or driving licence. Nothing. So how did we know her name? Because she had told the staff, verbally. So how do we even know this is her real name? The answer of course, is that we don't.

We didn't even have a photograph. I had a description, a name, and a date of birth. I wrote down all I could, including the names of the staff who had interacted with her.

I submitted the information into our missing persons database. I should have entered in the very obvious facts, known to me through my experience at the hospital. I knew for example, that there were no CCTV cameras in the ward. There are no cameras in any of the wards, actually. The nearest camera to this particular ward was downstairs in North Corridor. One of the main arterial routes in the hospital, and some distance from the stairs up to this ward. Nevertheless I was asked to research the CCTV cameras in and around the ward, in order to find an image of Ms Din. Nigel wasn't too pleased. I can always tell. Normally quite positive, and chirpy when I ask him a favour, this time he said something along the lines of: "What? North corridor? You're joking! No chance!" or words to that effect. I respected his judgment. But he looked anyway. Around the times she was thought to have initially been admitted and around the time she left. Plenty of people on the camera shuffling about, up and down. Lots of people. But Nathan, in typical form, and with a plan of the hospital obviously imprinted in his brain, pointed out there was more than one door to the outside between the foot of the stairwell, and where the camera was located. Not only that, there's a link corridor upstairs, connecting all the wards. She didn't even have to come down those particular stairs. So there's a real likelihood she wouldn't even pass that camera in North corridor. Little wonder we didn't find her, or anyone looking remotely like her description.

She'd given the ward staff an address. It was across the other side of the city. So I jumped into my van and drove over there. It was a rough part of town, with a high immigrant population and student accommodation. I knocked on the door. A young oriental chap answered, opening the door. Obviously a student. He looked worried when he saw me.

"Can I come in a minute please?" I asked, already halfway into the room.

"Can I help you?" the chap said, in barely recognisable English, still holding the door, as I was now standing in the front room. The house smelt of boiled rice, cooking fat, and incense. There was a small shrine, as is their custom, in one corner of the living room, with incense sticks surrounding it.

"Yes. I'm looking for Ms Din. Lin Su Din. Do you know her? I'm the hospital police officer."

I took hold of one corner of my hospital ID badge hanging from my stab vest, with the index finger and thumb of my left hand, and indicated for him to see it. He peered at it, leaning forward slightly, and his mouth falling open, as though I was showing him some sort of priceless antiquity.

"She's gone from the hospital. We need to know if she's okay. Do you understand me?"

He turned and started speaking in what I could only assume was Vietnamese, or similar, to someone at the back of the house, in the kitchen. A female voice came back at him, also, I guessed, in the same language. The reply was abrupt and stilted. I imagined a translation:

"Coppers? Tell him we know nothing! Get rid of him!"

There was a real likelihood, of course, that these people knew the missing person, or 'misper' as we call them. There was also a real possibility too that these people were illegal entrants into the country. Frankly I wasn't too concerned. I tried to explain this to them, as best I could, that I just wanted to see Ms Din, see she was fit and well, and I'd be on my way.

"She's missing from the hospital. She gave them this address. Do you know her?" I was probably coming across as being too desperate by this time. Then the owner of the voice from the kitchen appeared at the door. A young, attractive oriental woman with a tea-towel in her hands, drying a large dinner plate with it.

"Sorry. We don't know." She said, in good English. Her eyes didn't move from me and she looked at me as though I'd just challenged her to a staring competition. The male again said something to the woman in Vietnamese. I quickly ran through the description of the misper in my head. Long black hair. The date of birth indicated she would have been twenty years old. Slim. Oriental. Just like the woman standing a few feet from me now. I needed to know who these people were.

"Do you have any identification? A passport?"

They both looked at one another, with admirably blank expressions. She went back into the kitchen. She reappeared with a coat, and took some papers from one of the pockets and handed them to me. Amongst these papers was a Vietnamese passport. The photo was of her. The name was *not* Lin Su Din. Did I really think it would be that easy? Probably not.

I enjoyed missing from home enquiries and liked to pride myself on a reasonable record of success. My first one, years ago, was upsetting though. I spent almost a whole shift looking for a young lad in a part of the city which had a deservedly terrible reputation. I managed to find this lad and took him home. I was so relieved. He was a nice lad, only nine years old. He seemed to enjoy the ride in my police car back to where he lived. His dad answered the door. A tall, fat, unshaven monster of a man in a string vest. There was much evidence of numerous meals spilled down this vest on the strings, with food remains dried and matted into thick, greasy chest hair. He had a sandwich in one hand and a cigarette burning in the other. I said to him, in naïve excitement:

"I found him! Here he is!" as I gently ushered the lad into the house. The man's reply caught me completely by surprise, and saddened me to the extent that I remember the incident as clearly now as when it happened nearly thirty years ago:

"What you brought 'im back 'ere for? We don't fuckin' want 'im!"

But rules are rules and so I left him with his loving father and drove away.

Back in the search for the missing Vietnamese patient, I still hoped she may be in the house. It was quite a large terraced dwelling and I could do with having a good look around.

"Is there anyone else living here?" I asked, indicating to the stairs.

"No. No. You can see." She stood to one side obviously offering me the bottom of the stairs. I had to take this opportunity, while I was there. I usually do anyway, for whatever reason. I always accept someone's invitation to search their property with consent. I'm just inquisitive, I suppose!

I walked up the carpet-less stairs and heard them behind me chattering quickly together. He seemed far more concerned than she did. Her voice was calming, while he seemed to be getting more and more agitated. I looked in the three bedrooms and the bathroom. The rooms were virtually empty, with just one double mattress on the floor of one room. That was it. I didn't go in the loft. The loft hatch did not look used. It's sometimes easy to tell, with paint wear around the wood, and perhaps scuff marks on the walls. So I didn't look. I descended the stairs and rejoined them still standing where I'd left them.

"Thank you," I said, as I took out my pocket book. I wrote my details on a piece of paper and handed it to the woman. She folded it over and kept it in her hand. I walked to the door, opened it, and left. I wasn't happy about the situation. The next day I returned, early, with Gary. We knocked on the front door for several minutes. No-one answered. I went around the back and peered in through the kitchen window. There was no evidence of anyone living there. There was no food left out, no crockery, nothing. I tried again, later in the week, and still no-one answered. It seemed whoever it was I'd spoken to had gone.

We've had some contact with the Vietnamese Embassy about Ms Din. But they have also been unable to help. The same goes for the UK immigration authorities. We've checked all the local universities and colleges. All the hospitals in the region were also checked, in case she was readmitted anywhere. We even sent her toothbrush she left behind in the ward for DNA tests. It was tested, at great expense, but with a negative result. She'd obviously rinsed it under the tap after using it. Very inscrutable. Huge amounts of police time have been spent on this enquiry. All for nothing. The most annoying thing about the whole exercise is that this woman may not even be using her real name. As a consequence, even if we did find her, how would we know?

SHIFTY

I don't mean someone is behaving in a 'shifty' manner. Though this particular one did. 'Shifty' is the colloquial hospital name for the 'shift engineers'. There are dozens of them. In essence, they are the maintenance men. And they work shifts. Hence the nickname. I know most people on the campus work shifts of some sort, but this name has stuck, peculiarly, to them. If you've ever given it any thought, and you probably haven't, a hospital is obviously a very complex place, with masses of expensive equipment and machines and so on that could, and do, go wrong. Heating systems break down, doors need fixing, lights go out, trolleys lose wheels, chairs break. In fact any number of things can happen in a hospital where someone is needed to come along with a tool box and fix something. Twenty-four hours a day. This is the role of the shifties. They can put a shelf up for you, build a wall, make furniture, or indeed almost anything. As far as I know there are no female shifties, not yet anyway. Still very much a masculine preserve. They don't immediately fall into my list of possible thieves, as perhaps cleaners sometimes do. Why not? They have access to most places, day and night, and would be quite skilled with doors and locks, so perhaps they ought to go on such a list of suspects.

As usual with such light-fingered persons, the one and only shifty I've dealt with became greedy. If these thieves contented themselves with the very occasional theft, perhaps months, or even years apart, then they would prove quite difficult or even impossible to catch. But as I've stated already, the vast majority of them cannot resist expanding their activities. They seem to believe they are somehow immune from capture, probably because they have been doing it for so long. As in the case of this particular shifty.

A certain amount of material loss is acceptable and 'written off'. Every organization has to accept this. From paper clips and pencils to larger items of stationery. A huge place such as a hospital understandably has huge amounts of everything delivered and left lying around. Great numbers of people have worked there for years, even decades. Certain working practices have wormed their way into the daily life at the hospital. Some people may assume smaller items are free and available as a perk of the job. If only they kept to this, to these small items, instead of progressing to large ones, and worse still, stealing from colleagues and patients.

I was contacted directly on my police mobile phone by one of the shifty's line managers. I arranged to meet him at a quiet time, in his office. Reticence was written all over his face. Not surprising, really, as the man in question had seemingly worked there since God was a boy. He was well-liked too, at least by some. Others had already cast aspersions on his character. I do tend to find this sometimes. On arrival in a department where thieving has been taking place for a while, particularly highly emotive crime such as theft from work-mates and patients, I am sign-posted to the suspect by the offender's colleagues, clearly fed up with the person's behaviour. Strong hints have often already been made to warn the person, which are ignored. So it seems I am called as a desperate measure, often as an exasperated last resort.

I walked into the shift engineers' workshop via a heavy sliding door straight off the service road and into the wood-working area. Large work-benches scattered with tools and saw-dust, the room pungent with a strong wood and glue smell, reminiscent of my days long ago in school woodworking, which I was rubbish at. There was a calendar on the wall with a large-breasted, topless woman with long blonde hair and huge saucer-like nipples smiling out from it as 'Miss February'. Racks of tools hung in neat rows on the walls and a small radio on a bench in the corner was straining a current top twenty hit across the otherwise empty room. I walked down a corridor and found another corridor off to my left. Then a door, propped open with a bit of scrap wood, and a chap in late middle-age sat at a computer, looking intently at the screen.

"Mike?" I said, as I walked in, removing my big pointy hat.

"Yes, come in, get yourself a seat," he said, peering over the top of his spectacles at me. He continued one-finger typing, with the index finger of his right hand. I saw him tap the 'enter' key very heavily and decisively as though setting off World War Three with it and a pleased expression fell across his face. He suddenly stood up and kicked the piece of wood away from under the door before shutting it with a deft movement of his left hand, and sitting back in his chair.

"Thanks for coming in. I just need some advice."

"It's nice and warm in here," I commented, removing my leather gloves, and stuffing them inside my helmet. I took hold of a chair at another unoccupied desk and drew it up closer to where Mike was sitting. I've always found people in these circumstances usually do initially ask for 'advice' from me, rather than, 'There's a colleague here who's stealing and I want you to arrest them.' Though of course this is frequently the end result.

"We've got a problem with stuff going missing. Not just the usual stuff, but Derek's had some money go missing yesterday off his desk." He indicated to the desk my chair had belonged to, obviously where Derek usually sits.

"And we've had lottery money go too. And other things. One lad's watch has gone from his work bench." Mike opened a drawer and started sifting through some papers.

"I made a list of all the things that's been happening, for my benefit as much as anything," he said, finally passed me a hand-written note with a dozen things listed on it. 'Kettle (chrome, cordless, brand new). Toaster (chrome, new). Ladders (aluminium, new). Paint (light green, emulsion, six large tins). Tools. Phone. £200 cash. Lottery – about £35. Tea bags. Coffee. Watch (Seiko, gents, digital). Keys. Batteries (all sizes, including several new car batteries).'

I saw the 'ladders' on the list. Ladders? How on earth would someone steal a set of ladders, unseen?

"How big are these ladders, do you know?" I said, in an obviously curious tone.

"Yes. They were brand new, about six weeks ago. I ordered them myself and can describe them very well. The make, colour, and everything. Aluminium ones, folding. They were quite expensive too."

"When did they disappear then?" I said, scanning the list.

"Not long after they arrived. I don't think anyone here even had the chance to use them. I had to order another set, which arrived a few weeks ago. I keep *them* locked away."

I could see Mike was looking at me while I read the list, expecting a comment.

"Blimey" I said. "Quite a mixture of stuff. When did this start?"

"It's been going on for months. But Derek's two hundred quid went missing yesterday, off his desk, there. Yesterday afternoon. I think I know who took it too. I'm not sure about all of the other stuff, but… well, it's not for me to say is it, really?"

Mike's voice tapered off toward the end, uncertain and hesitant.

"Where's Derek now?" I asked, looking around the room, as though he'd be hiding under a desk.

"He's off today. The money was part of a collection he'd been sorting out for someone else. He's gutted. Well, we all are. But I think I know who took it."

"Why, what happened?" I said fishing for anything remotely resembling useable evidence.

"Ron, Ron Hutchinson, one of the blokes, came in the office yesterday afternoon and was standing at Derek's desk talking to him and telling some crappy jokes, like he does. He thinks he's a real comedian. He was stood there for ages. The money was just loose on the desk, right where he was standing. Derek was up and down all the time, he wasn't really paying him any notice. It was around then that the money disappeared. There was no-one else at Derek's desk yesterday. Not as far as I can remember. There was only me and him in here."

"Right," I said. I touched my face with my left hand, thoughtfully, and rubbed my chin. 'I missed a bit this morning when I shaved,' I thought, momentarily distracted from the work in hand and passed the list back to Mike.

"Can I have a copy of this? Have you got a photo-copier?" I asked.

Mike spun his chair around, without saying anything, and turned to his right. A small copying machine sat on a cupboard behind his desk. He lifted the lid and pressed the button. The light flashed left to right, it hummed and whirred for a few seconds, then he opened it and handed me the copy.

"The other things," Mike said, drawing my attention as I folded the list into my pocket book.

"The other things on the list have all gone missing when Ron's been at work. When he's been on lates, usually on his own. It's not for me to say, but you know what I mean?"

I understood what Mike was saying. This was another example of one member of a team going bad. A rotten apple in a basket of otherwise decent fruit. If fifty men are mainly honest and hard-working, and one of them starts thieving, it can become clear, given sufficient time, and incidents, who the individual may be. I thanked Mike and walked back through the workshop and out into the service road. I began working out a plan of attack. As usual the best place to strike is at the home address.

Two days later, at five-thirty in the morning, I was driving the big van to one of the outer suburbs of the city. Gary was in the front next to me, highly critical of my driving, as usual, and with two more colleagues in the back. I don't drive police vehicles beyond the speed limits any more. It's extremely stressful. We're not exempt from road traffic law either, so I don't run the risk. I usually let Gary drive. If I don't, as in this case, I am bombarded with endearing comments such as:

"For fuck's sake, grand-dad, get a move on..!" and so on, expressing his obvious frustration. He has a certain unique way with his words, does our Gary.

Eventually, despite my slow driving, we pulled up outside, jumped out and I locked the doors. I approached Ron's front door and knocked loudly. It was still very dark and there were no lights from inside. I knocked again. An upstairs front bedroom light came on and curtains moved. A few moments later Ron answered the door:

"What's going on? What's wrong?" he said, obviously just woken up from a deep sleep.

"Ron I'm the hospital police officer. I need to come in and speak to you for a moment."

"Yes I know I've seen you before. What's this about?" he replied, just as he opened the door wider, I assumed to allow us in.

I stepped inside his house just as a woman, presumably his wife, was walking down the stairs in her dressing gown. Gary and my other two colleagues followed me in.

"You are under arrest on suspicion of theft from the hospital." I said to him. He didn't say anything. He didn't look particularly surprised either. I sat them both down in the living room. I stood there and looked around the room. I could smell fresh paint. The walls in the lounge were a fresh light green shade, obviously recently painted, and looked really well applied, as though by a professional. It reminded me of how my own house was in need of some similar treatment. But enough of this. I had to find some evidence. Ron was not saying anything at that stage, and neither was his wife. He just kept looking at his digital watch on his wrist, rather nervously I thought.

I walked through into the kitchen. A shiny new toaster sat on a work surface next to an equally shiny looking cordless kettle. Near the back door there were two large car batteries next to a large wicker laundry basket. The basket was full of toilet rolls. There must have been a hundred or more. I took out my spectacles and picked one up to take a closer look. Each one had 'HOSPITAL PROPERTY' written through it like seaside rock. I opened a cupboard and saw roll upon roll of large plastic bin bags each one with the same 'HOSPITAL PROPERTY' screaming out at me. The cupboards were full of industrial size cleaning products, the likes of which I've never seen in the shops. But things I'd frequently seen in and around the hospital.

Gary shouted from upstairs. I'd given them each a copy of Mike's list. I went up the stairs and one of the bedrooms was obviously being decorated. Pale green paint tins on the floor, a set of sparkling new aluminium ladders set up in the bedroom to help access those difficult, harder-to-reach places. Hospital overalls were draped over the banister. A doctor's stethoscope was hanging in a bedroom wardrobe. Beautiful shelves everywhere in the house, in almost every room, just like the ones I'd seen in so many doctors' offices. There were some limited edition prints on the walls in expensive aluminium frames similar to those I'd seen hanging in South Corridor until quite recently. I went inside the attached garage and saw the most comprehensive private collection of hand tools and power tools I think I have ever seen. All neatly arranged and hanging from the walls.

Of course we'd walked into an Aladdin's Cave. We scarcely had enough room in the van, despite its size. Ron actually helped us to box it all up and carry it to the van, in between constantly mumbling, "I've been set up... I've been set up." I took the watch off him. Well, once he realised his situation, he handed it to me himself.

He admitted it all. Apart from the thefts which had finally drawn the most attention to himself, the missing money. I couldn't prove he'd taken it, either. He continued to allege that somehow, someone had 'set him up'. Not really Ron. No-one forced him to part-furnish and decorate his whole house with hospital property. He didn't even have to pay to wipe his backside! He refused to tell me why he took the stethoscope and why it was hanging in his bedroom. Perhaps him and his wife had been enjoying playing 'doctors and nurses' when alone at weekends. We do find some strange things sometimes when searching people's houses. No other profession would be in this privileged a position as to reveal a person's most intimate secrets. In one bedroom once, on another occasion, a colleague found a very large rubber penis with a suction cup on the base, hidden deep inside a bedroom drawer. He stuck it to the wall, complete with remnants of pubic hair still attached. Very unprofessional.

Ron was dismissed, as per usual procedure. But because we'd recovered most of the property in good condition, he escaped prison. He left the city for a new life elsewhere.

BARRY'S GHOST

On occasions when discussing the content of this book with my friends in the hospital security team, I was asked if I knew anything of Barry's ghost. 'No, no-one's told me,' I replied, and so became curious and eager to find out more. The next time I was on the campus I asked Barry to call in the office to tell me about it. Barry is a decent chap. God-fearing and obviously quite religious. His faith is important to him. Not only is this quite evident when talking to him, but he will tell you so himself. Strange that he'd never told me, and no-one else had, until I informed him I was collecting such anecdotes for this book. He swore it was true. So who am I to accuse a God-fearing man of lying?

Just off North Road there were some old doctors' accommodation blocks, now demolished and completely rebuilt. It was in one of these where the Swedish doctor had lived, the one claiming to have been systematically poisoned. It was a long time before the old buildings were demolished. Years in fact. In the meantime they had to be guarded, virtually night and day, to prevent the obvious vandalism and thefts, and so on. The modern trend nowadays when a building of any size becomes empty is for it to be immediately and speedily demolished and carted away in lorries, rather than prolonging the agony of emptiness at continued great expense. The block consisted of around fifty separate rooms and a general office on the ground floor at the end of a long corridor, with rooms off each side. As the flats emptied, the ground floor office was kept available to members of the security team to use when on their rounds. There was power, light, a kettle and even a small television.

One very quiet Sunday afternoon, as Barry described it, he made his way along North Road, up the few steps and into the building. It was a warm afternoon, he let himself in with the key, and started to have a quick look around. He checked the alarm system, and deactivated the one small zone where he would be sitting for a while. The rest of the building was now unoccupied and the alarm was live. He made himself a cup of tea and placed it on the small table in the office. He knew there was a match on the television, so he switched it on and sat back down. It was only a small black and white tv, but he was excited at the prospect of being able to watch it, or at least *some* of it. His local team was playing at home and they were doing very well, unlike more recent times! Barry sipped his tea and became quite engrossed in the match. It was still nil-nil by the time he'd finished his mug of tea. He thought how hungry he was, as he'd been on duty since six that morning, and it was by then mid-afternoon and he'd not had any lunch.

After about twenty minutes he heard the first bang. He turned the television down a touch and turned his head towards where he thought he'd heard the noise. Nothing. He turned the tv back up, slightly, but not as loud as before. As he did so there came another bang from the same direction as the last one. It sounded as though it had come from way down the corridor, at the far end of the building. He could see the alarm panel on the wall near the door and saw all the lights lit, indicating the system was active, but nothing had been triggered. So there was no-one there. But then there was another *bang!* from down the corridor, this time much louder, as though something had fallen or been pushed over. He turned the television right down and listened again. There was more banging. He stood up and went to the door. He stepped into the corridor and looked down the building. Suddenly the banging grew in intensity and sounded like someone was smashing the place up. Barry told me it sounded as though someone was slamming an object down hard onto the floor or bashing something against a wall, or onto a desk. The noise was getting louder as though coming towards him. But there was nothing there! I asked Barry if there were kids on the roof fetching a football, or banging on the walls or windows, but he said not. It was daylight and there was no-one around.

As the noise grew closer it began to sound like someone fighting and being hurled around. There was then a dragging sound which Barry states sounded so very real he imagined it close enough to swallow him up completely at any moment. The noise was right there, a few feet in front of him. Something being dragged, heavy and cumbersome, towards him, as though now almost on top of him. But still there was nothing there that he could see. Barry decided he would turn and run. He made the decision to turn and get out of the building. He just wanted to get out. This wasn't right. He could hear all these things coming at him, but there was nothing there! This couldn't be real! But his legs failed to respond and his body remained fixed to the floor. He couldn't even move his arms. This had never happened to him before and has never happened since. He felt ice cold and utterly, utterly alone. A few seconds into his paralyzed state he managed to turn and run. He actually ran from the building as though being chased for all his life by a wild animal.

An hour later two of Barry's colleagues returned and checked the whole building together. There was no sign of any forced entry and no damage anywhere inside the building. Barry swore it sounded as though the whole place was being smashed up. But there was nothing.

You may dismiss Barry's account and even laugh. But allow me to tell you something of the building's history. Years before, when it was fully occupied, one of the tenants, a young student doctor, had returned to his room in a very agitated state. He'd apparently been drinking heavily and was known to be depressed. He locked himself in his room and continued drinking. He was apparently heard muttering things to himself, punctuated with occasional loud shouts, according to people in the other rooms nearby. Then there was the sound of smashing from in his room as though he was throwing things around violently, reaching a crescendo after a few minutes then suddenly going very quiet. His neighbours couldn't get in the room. The door was locked. The manager was called and he couldn't open the door either, as the key was still in the lock. Eventually the police and fire brigade were called. They forced their way in with huge difficulty. The young doctor was hanging by his neck from the ceiling. He'd bashed a hole in the roof space in order to anchor a rope around a thick steel joist. Not only that, he'd dragged most of his furniture from all around the flat, even the washing machine from the kitchen area, and piled it up against the door. He'd really meant to do it. He'd finally smashed everything else up, before kicking a stool away from under him. His room was directly above the end of the corridor where Barry had been standing.

LIES

So I am nearing the end of my walking tour of the campus and am now back at the HQ Building, having gone full circle . Years ago before I became the hospital cop, the only time I would ever enter the grounds was on the advice of, and in company with a colleague, now retired, who wanted to ogle the nurses lying on the grass at the rear of the nurses' home building, as it was then. On hot days they would sit in small groups reading, or sunbathing, scantily clad, unaware they were being watched by a pervy old police officer and me. Today the building is the Headquarters and most of the grass at the back is given over to car parking. But there's still some lawn to sit on and a grassy bank quite pleasant in the shade of several mature trees, preserved when the car park was laid. I was about to walk into the building via the back doors one warm summer afternoon when I stopped to chat to a young man sitting on this grass bank adjacent to the car park.

It was a very hot afternoon and I was close to finishing work. He seemed quite amenable, so I took off my big hat and sat down on the grass next to him. He was taking occasional gulps from a half-bottle of Scotch. I then noticed a bottle of tablets in his other hand.

"What's your name, young man?" I asked him, trying to see what else he might have to hand.

"Kyle. Kyle Carter." He replied, matter-of-factly. He took another swig and stared ahead, somewhere off into the distance.

"What's going on, Kyle, what are you up to? I mean, I'm just curious. Why are you sitting here, drinking? It's not the usual place to come and sit, and spend time drinking, is it?"

He turned his head slowly and said nothing. He took out some tobacco and started to roll a cigarette. He wasn't doing it very well and tobacco was falling through his hands into the grass. He pecked at it with his fingers in a vain attempt to retrieve the loss.

"It's a lovely day, eh?" I said, trying to tease a response from him. "Too hot to sit here…you're in the grounds of a hospital, you know. What are you doing here?" I said.

"I'm just chillin'" he said, demurely, continuing to look blank.

"What's that in your hand?" I asked, pointing at the small plastic bottle in his right hand.

"Tablets," he replied. "I've just taken a load of 'em."

"Not a good idea was it?" I said, winning first prize in the 'Stating the Bleeding Obvious' contest.

"Let me see," I said as I took the bottle from his hand, rather snatchingly and without much in the way of prior consent. I read the label and confess I'd never heard of the very long brand name on the bottle. So I asked him:

"What do these do?"

"Dunno. They're me mam's. I just took 'em… with this." The half bottle of Scotch was now almost completely drained. He tried lighting his cigarette but the lighter wouldn't work. Just my luck, I thought, to find this idiot sitting here like this. I called up on my radio and asked for a name check. If he lived locally, I could shout a colleague and we could take him home. Or even to admissions, if he really had taken the tablets he said he had. Then leave him there. I didn't know what the tablets were, but they probably wouldn't be doing him any good, to say the least. The voice of the female control operator came back to me with a result of the name check:

"Yes, he's whiskey mike times two, over…"

Shit. 'Whiskey mike' means 'WANTED/MISSING' for something. Twice.

I readied my speed-cuffs, but looking at him he didn't seem in any state to either run off or put up a fight of any sort. Usually if a person is wanted by the police they know full well what it is about. So I asked him:

"Kyle. You're wanted. Twice. What's it for?"

"Oh that," he said, leaning back on the grass, and staring up at the sky. "I nicked me dad's credit card and went off with it for a while. That was last year..!"

I shouted for a car and two colleagues pulled up a few minutes later. I should have called an ambulance instead. He was visibly wilting in front of my eyes. I couldn't take him into police custody in this state. He'd never pass the health check questions. We don't take anyone in to our care any longer who is in any way ill, or even extremely drunk. It's always the worst publicity for the police service for someone to die in custody. There seems to be an automatic assumption by some in the media, and those in the public who hate us, for their own reasons, that the person must have been mercilessly beaten to death by wicked, evil, Nazi police officers. In my Force there have been less than half a dozen in the last thirty years. All had either a very serious pre-existing health complaint, or were blind drunk. Or both. So we don't accept people in that state any more. I've never, ever, seen a detainee subjected to assault by police officers, other than lawful self-defence and restraint on the part of the police. So we took Kyle to casualty.

I stood with him in casualty for hours. He was periodically checked over by a nurse. In the meantime I was stranded in his company, marooned on this island of irredeemable despondency. I asked him about his past. He was a thin lad, imbued with a preponderance of aphoristic knowingness which belied his youthful twenty-four years. He'd been in the army, he said, and served in Afghanistan, no less, and returned after six months badly affected by PTSD, Post Traumatic Stress Disorder. He'd seen mates step on land mines and had shot and killed Afghan civilians. He was suffering repeated nightmares and found it difficult to readapt back into mainstream society. Apparently. What he hadn't done, you wouldn't want to do. He'd been anywhere you'd been, twice. He'd done everything you'd done, or ever thought of doing. And it had all become too much for him. So he was now engaged in a spiral of self-destructiveness, or so it seemed, due to his rueful inability to cope with his present circumstances. I asked if he'd sought any help, but he said he hadn't. He went on a crime spree at the end of the previous year when he took the credit card, and said he was relieved it would all be over and dealt with soon.

After four hours of listening to this man's short but very hectic and challenging life story, a doctor finally came to see him. I left the cubicle so he could have a private consultation with him. Ten minutes later the doctor came back out.

"We're going to have to keep him in," he said to me. I was elated that I wasn't going to have to stay with this man any longer.

"Why?" I asked, in perfunctory concern.

"Because he's telling me he's suicidal. He'll need referring and keeping in for his own safety."

"Oh, right," I said to the young doctor. "I'll bail him from here to see me at a later date then," I said. 'Street bail' as it's known. A brilliant idea. I rang the custody sergeant at my police station on my police Blackberry and he agreed. He did not want him in his care anyway, that's for sure.

So I left him at the hospital. As a courtesy, before I went off duty I called in to the address he'd given, mainly because it was close to the police station. He was apparently living with his sister. This much, at least, was true. I was invited in by his sister Fiona and her boyfriend Dave. I told them briefly about the circumstances which led to his detention at the hospital and our conversations regarding his wartime traumas.

"What a load of rubbish..!" Dave extorted. "He's *such* an idiot!"

He could see I was listening intently and so I replied: "Really? Which bit?"

"ALL of it!" his sister interjected, firmly. "He's *never* been in the army. He's never been abroad. He doesn't even have a passport! What a load of rubbish! He nicked dad's credit card last year, that bit's true. He told me that was all sorted out, and the police weren't after him any more. The lying bastard! But trauma? What bloody trauma? The only problem he's got is he's an idle lying bastard!"

He answered his 'street bail' two weeks later and I charged him with several offences relating to his dad's credit card. I pondered as to why a person makes up such stories, at such length and in such elaborate detail. Why would anyone want to fantasize about their life to this extent? The answer is of course they feel, for whatever reason, their real lives are perhaps too feckless an existence, denuded of structure and fulfilment, and the need to embellish them fills these chasms in their existence. But when one encounters such a person, after a while it becomes clear that anything they then say has to be treated with the utmost suspicion. In the end, a conversation with them feels empty, unrewarding, and pointless, as any replies given are virtually worthless.

NORTH RD
LOOKING EAST

EPILOGUE

So now you know some of my activities at the hospital. I'm not there every day, but most days when I'm on duty. It is only a third of my beat area, after all! As I write this I'm still a serving officer. I may well be walking around the hospital campus tomorrow, in my bright fluorescent coat and big pointy hat. You might see me there, and I might engage you in polite conversation, too, and give you one or two of my stock replies I talked about! At any moment when on duty I may be asked to do anything from sort out a suspicious bag, to investigate a complex series of thefts in a busy department. I'd done some very different jobs before I joined the police service. I once worked in a chicken slaughterhouse. I submitted my resignation after two hours, in the first coffee break actually, but the management insisted I work a full week. It was awful. I'd worked in a bank for a while. I spent most of my time there day-dreaming about stealing some of the great piles of money in the vault, rather than concentrating on the work. It was so very crushingly boring! I lived and worked abroad for several years. Picking fruit, selling stuff door-to-door, labouring: Whatever I could get. But I have to say, after all that, a job in the police service has to be the best I've ever had. By far.

ACKNOWLEDGMENTS

I need to thank all the staff at the hospital for the source material in this book. From the cleaners to the Chief Executive. Colleagues in the police, such as Gary, of course, and others who helped in these incidents. Also my own force for tolerating me, my efforts, and this book. A massive thank you goes to the security staff at the hospital. Nigel, Julie, Shaun, Barry, Tony, John, Nathan (both Nathans!), Martin, Andy and all the team. Including those no longer there such as Ron and Mark. Huge amounts of work is involved in keeping a place like a hospital safe, so it is a credit to them all that despite its size, it remains one of the safest places in the city.

This hospital is not unique. I am sure the same, or very similar things happen in your own local hospital all the time. It's just that you will hardly ever get to hear about it. You may see the occasional doctor or other member of the medical profession splashed across the media when in court for one reason or another. And don't forget the wrong-doers I've dealt with are a very tiny proportion of the people working there. There are around five thousand members of staff in my hospital. In the last six years I've had to deal with only twelve of them.

As I write this, the public sector in the UK is undergoing huge changes. The biggest of which is job cuts. The majority of public sector workers, particularly in the Health Service work extremely hard, undertaking some very unpleasant tasks which we, the rest of us, would never consider doing. The greatest of all acknowledgements therefore goes to them.

Pc Jonathan Nicholas
Feb 2011